DO YOU KNOW THE HOLY GHOST?
THE SILENT WHISPER

Jesus

Ryan Cann

Do You Know The Holy Ghost? The Silent Whisper "Jesus"

By Ryan Matthias Cann Sr.

1st Edition 2020

ISBN 978-1-7357176-0-9 (Paperback Edition)

ISBN 978-1-7357176-1-6 (eBook Edition)

ISBN 978-1-7357176-3-0 (Audio Edition)

ISBN 978-1-7357176-5-4 (Hardback Edition)

Library of Congress Control Number2020917248

Editing by Mary Hoekstra

Front Cover Image by Bruce Rolff

Printed and bound in the United States of America

First Printing November 2020

Published by Father's Way Publishing LLC

Marrero, LA

Visit www.FathersWay143.com

Dedication

To all of Our Father's children who may be looking for

a beacon of light, and to all of those shining bright.

Table of Contents

Preface

Matthew 6:

9) After this manner, therefore, pray ye: Our Father which art in heaven, Hallowed be thy name. **10)** Thy kingdom come. Thy will be done on earth, as it is in heaven. **11)** Give us this day our daily bread. **12)** And forgive us our debts, as we forgive our debtors. **13)** And lead us not into temptation but deliver us from evil: For thine is the kingdom and the power, and the glory, forever. Amen. **14)** For if ye forgive men their trespasses, your heavenly Father will also forgive you: **15)** But if ye forgive not men their trespasses, neither will your Father forgive your trespasses.

Acts 19:

1) And it came to pass, that, while Apollos was at Corinth, Paul having passed through the upper coasts came to Ephesus: and finding certain disciples, **2)** He said unto them, Have ye received the Holy Ghost since ye believed? And they said unto him, We have not so much as heard whether there be any Holy Ghost. **3)** And he said unto them, Unto what then were ye baptized? And they said, Unto John's baptism. **4)** Then said Paul, John verily baptized with the baptism of repentance, saying unto the people, that they should believe on him which should come after him, that is, on Christ Jesus. **5)** When they heard this, they were baptized in the name of the Lord Jesus.

*I hope this book fulfills
its intended purpose
of introducing you
to The Holy Spirit/Holy Ghost.*

Ryan M. Cann, Sr.

Editor's Foreword

The message Ryan Cann clearly states in this first book is simple: "Once we acknowledge how we naturally think and admit that our thinking operates with animosity towards God, the truth of life comes rushing in." The truth that rushes in, if we acknowledge how to invite and welcome it, is the Holy Spirit and all that the Holy Spirit within us conveys and promises, as it lives in us.

Since you're reading this book, you probably know at least the basics of all those aspects of Christian salvation, so Ryan goes deeper. He shares his own journey toward knowing the Holy Spirit and states how critical it is to recognize that our thoughts and subsequent actions are carnal. Those carnal thoughts and actions are in opposition to God Our Father, and we are in opposition to God through our own choices.

Neither God Our Father, nor the Holy Spirit, move nor hide or dodge us; God and the Holy Spirit do not avoid us, repudiate us, or cut us off. Jesus died where all could see; He certainly fulfilled the Will of God and His teachings yet abide. We are the ones who do the hiding, dodging, avoiding, repudiating, and severing of contact with Our Father, Our Savior, and the Holy Spirit. We start approaching God and seeking the Holy Spirit by seeking His mercy and grace. Those are realistic goals, but they require work on our lives, thoughts, behaviors, and worldly lives. Ryan says "Someone who is ready to get past grace and mercy, is ready to surpass doing the minimum in life. Our Father wants more than our minimum. He wants our all."

Ryan, in what I've called his "going 10 rounds with God," shares his blunt, straightforward dialogues with Our Father, just as he knows all of us do! Ryan tosses up every reason, excuse, lame-brain logic, reluctance, resistance, and self-righteous barrier he has ever used to challenge God in his life. It's a lose-win bout for him at first, so Ryan does some soul-searching, some Scripture-studying, a lot of thinking and questioning, and even tries to pose new arguments and points of debate. And then, he surrenders.

Ryan writes, "At the moment I realized, in trying to become the best Ryan I could be, I became the worst version of the Holy Spirit. I became non-present in Spirit. Ryan was, and forever will be tainted with the lust of the eye...the things that pull at my pride, ego, and vanity. I had to learn, as I blindly accepted before, that Ryan and Our Father cannot exist at the same time. It is either going to be me or Our Father leading the decision-making process...thinking. I realized I forgot to renew my mind. I forgot to say, 'I am stupid; You are smart. I am foolish; You are wise. I am the sinner; You are my salvation.'"

And so we may all realize. Ryan continues, "I had to wash all my thinking and thoughts against what I knew our Father would want me to do. I realized that my Father does not care about worldly possessions. He cares about the transgressions we are committing towards Him and each other. He wants us to spread love. Therefore, if we succumb to measuring life by man's judgments and measurements, we are already using the wrong scale. Our Father wants us to be held accountable to love. Our Father measures a successful day by whether we were charitable, positive, and helpful to our fellow man. Until we admit we should operate in perfection, we will never attain operating in our Father's Spirit."

Inviting the Holy Spirit into our lives does require deep changes in how we live, interact with one another and with those whom we do not know, and having the strength of our faith. We must live in Charity. Our actions reflect and are built upon Charity, and if we are able to put on "the white robe" of the Holy Spirit in us, we will not only be in the fullness of Our Father and Savior, but we also will be in the fullness of the Body of Christ on Earth.

It was an honor, a privilege, a struggle, and a joy to work with Ryan on "Do You Know the Holy Spirit." I look forward to re-reading this book, just as I look forward (and so should you) to finding out what comes next!

Mary Hoekstra, Editor
5 August 2020

DAY
ONE
TAKING THE FIRST STEP

Getting to Know God

It was a normal day off at Forward Operating Base (FOB) Ghazni in Afghanistan. I got a fast start to the day. My laundry was in the dryer. The shower after my morning workout had just given me life, and I was ready to enjoy getting to do nothing all day. I stopped by the small coffee shop next to the basketball courts to smoke a cigar, as I waited for my clothes to finish.

I ordered a large coffee and started lighting my cigar. I was happy to have the day off. Relaxing and decompressing from the six, twelve-hour shifts was all that was on my agenda. As I waited on the cup of coffee, my mind began to wander as I thought to myself, *What is life about? Why do we exist? Is there any real meaning to life? Is there any truth in all this nonsense?*

I began to take in my surroundings. Army personnel was all around me, but the women were catching my attention the most.

Hey, forgive me. It's Afghanistan. There aren't many women out here, and a couple look real…

RYAN! I caught myself. *How do you expect to learn and grow into anything more if you keep staring at these women?"* I had to accept the ultimate truth, *"I can't."*

My conscience and I have always gone round for round ever since I was young. I am a realist. The realness of any situation is always in the truth and the facts, never the emotions and feelings. I questioned whether looking at the female anatomy of strangers was worth losing everything. I was quick to admit to myself; it wouldn't be. The voice of truth added, *Well, then, why do you still do it?*

BOOOOM!!!

I looked around, shocked and confused, searching for answers. I felt the vibrations of it all, before I ever heard a sound. I immediately set my attention on where the vibrations were coming from, only to see an explosion happening right before my eyes. It wasn't like I expected, and nothing like anything anyone had told me before. Time slowed down to one frame at a time. Incoming images were slowly but rapidly approaching me, millisecond by millisecond. Before I could think, I dropped to the floor. My military training automatically took over. At a moment's notice, I was face down on the ground barely turning my head away in time, before it was ripped to shreds by broken pieces of glass and debris.

At that moment, it was easy to see how easy life can change in a moment's notice. When the realism of the fragility of life hits you, you automatically start to question life's ultimate purpose. I had sincerely asked a question; little did I know that the answers were soon to come. I sat in a bunker, gunfire and explosions in the distance by now. Thank God, I thought to myself. A few moments later, the mention of suicide bombers being on base came over the loudspeakers, and my intense stare turned to the local Afghani shop owner.

The voice of truth was quick to asked me, *"Ryan, I thought you stood for me; How has life put you in a position where you are ready to kill someone when yesterday you would have said he was a friend?"* I realized quickly the lessons given to me growing up had been replaced with something different. I remembered all the people who claimed I would be a great man of God one day. I had a choice to make. The only way their hopes could ever become true would be for me to at least try. I knew I had to start the process. I decided whatever process I had to begin; I would do it that day.

I was raised in the Church. The Bible wasn't foreign to me. I led Bible studies previously, and I knew I could preach if I had to. However, I never wanted to misinform someone of anything, so I knew I had to humble myself before God in order to receive His Word and teachings. Before committing to reading the Bible again, I said a small prayer. *God, I don't know anything. You know everything. Help me just read and not lean on my own understanding. Help me to actually take in the story and message, as opposed to just getting through the pages. Amen.*

The Bible took off, took over, and took life in me. I started to question everything I knew. I found out the Bible was a totally different story than all the preachers, pastors, evangelists, and prophets had ever told me. I learned that as loving as I thought I was in some ways, I was just as hateful in others. I learned that the only reason I was loving in certain areas was that I had chosen to listen to what I already knew to be right in those areas. *That's right. Listen!* came the voice I knew all too well. From now on, when the inner truth speaks, I will just use all caps. .

As I started to relearn everything I thought I had learned, I was able to fill in gaps I hadn't known were there. I realized that life can speed us up so much that we barely get a chance to think and reflect. I started to become more appreciative of being in Afghanistan. I had the time to look at myself in the mirror. I was able to soul-search without the distractions of the media, TV shows, news, movies, or anything else for that matter.

When I reached the New Testament, the greatest growth took place. I started to hold Bible studies with themes, as opposed to focusing on selected passages. The themes included questions like: Whose reward am I after? Is pride good? Can anger and rage give you an advantage? Then I came across the concept of charity. I changed everything I was doing and shifted the spotlight to love, with questions like: Can you forgive without forgetting? How can you remember someone hurting you if you can't keep a record of wrongs? How can you always trust?

I quickly started to realize that it was impossible to balance everything God had placed on me. I began to get angry at myself for not being able to perform the will of God like I wanted to, like I felt He wanted me to. Then my life took another turn when I read Romans chapter 7. I thought Paul was writing directly to me, as if he understood me! I understood that I was not the only one who knew what to do but sometimes found performing it impossible. Then Romans Chapter 8 hit me like a ton of bricks. *The Spirit,* I thought to myself, *Why hasn't the Spirit been touched on and highlighted like everything else?*

To get to know who we are, we have to be willing to accept what the truth reveals to us. The perception of truth is one of the biggest obstacles most people encounter when trying to understand who they are. All of us want to be able to identify ourselves with "good" and therefore, most of us try to attach ourselves to "good" by any means. The trick of life is to understand and shift our frame of reference. For us to understand who we are, we have to understand who God is. For us to understand who we are, we have to understand who God is.

Everyone wants to be able to identify with the good they do in their lives, as a part of themselves and their behavior. By us all wanting to believe ourselves to be good persons, we choose to look at our good and overlook our bad. We highlight the good in our lives, as opposed to paying attention to the "few" bad traits about ourselves. We don't want to accept the reality that the bad that appears in our lives is because of our own bad behavior traits, not just random acts or sudden rash decisions. We all want to distance ourselves from bad decision-making and negativity, so we often reject the trends life shows us about ourselves. We see bad choices as single occurrences, not lifelong practices. Our wanting to seem good, and therefore valuable in our own eyes, comes from us never wanting to accept who brings the bad into the equation.

Until we are willing to accept that the only good in life comes from God, we will never be willing to accept that the bad in life comes from us. Once we accept that we are flesh and blood with faults and weaknesses, we realize that we are automatically tied to sin. Therefore, we are tied to the devil. When we can accept that connection, we can see why we are always going to bring the bad and negativity to the equation.

We so often want to appear good enough in our own thoughts and judgments, that we forget God is trying to change us into something better. The key word is change. If we are changing into good, we must be something other than good. We like to look outwardly versus inwardly. Doing so allows us to be able to justify our faults. The more faults we can find in others, the less faulty we appear to ourselves. We have to remember that we can justify our wrongs to the point of no longer recognizing them. If we no longer recognize them, we cannot disown them. This is the carnal mind, and it is enmity against God. Enmity means *main opposition* and *foe*. Therefore, we must repent from this negative and hateful thinking. The more faults we can find in others, the less faulty we appear to ourselves.

Once we acknowledge how we naturally think and admit that our thinking operates with animosity towards God, the truth of life comes rushing in. We understand that God is God alone. Therefore, we can feel anything someone wants us to feel as an individual outside of God's direction and guidance. The more we identify with something, or place some form of identity on ourselves, the less we will be able to adapt and realize that we are anything and everything. By holding onto the pieces, we forget that we are the whole. This can be as simple as defining how we look to ourselves. Once we accept a certain look, we omit all other ways we can look and appear to others. In contrast, on a spiritual level, we can admit by holding on to ourselves as individuals, we are refusing to accept our role as a piece of the whole Body of Christ. Everything becomes confusing, and nothing seems to be truthful. There are too many single truths. We have been taught to live something out as individuals when it is meant to be received as a group.

Therefore, if society as a whole accepts something as the truth, we as individuals continue to evaluate what the whole accepts as the truth, compared to what we know and feel the truth is. We think to ourselves, *If this is the truth, then that must be a lie, but if that is a lie, everybody can't be lying. I must be the one not getting something. Let me go and reconsider all my truths, so I can see where I went wrong.* Then our minds go out and redefine the truth, so all the lies we now recognize make sense. Then, for the sake of fitting in, many allow lies to be redefined as the truth because the majority of people accept it. Political correctness is a prime example of this. This is one of the many ways the devil imposes on the will of God.

We learn to do this over and over in life to spare ourselves from the feelings the truth brings us. We don't want to admit to being disobedient. We blame everything but ourselves and our thinking. We convince ourselves to accept that this is the most that we can do. We keep our egos intact to the best of our abilities. We always want to be able to feel as if we can conquer this puzzle called life. We constantly look for ways to improve so we can defeat a current obstacle, only to find another obstacle waiting for us. We have a way of wanting to feel every self-satisfying trait out there, to feel happy about ourselves.

We fail to see that this is all a part of the devil's scheme. The enemy influences us to not want to admit nor acknowledge the entire truth. We never accurately measure ourselves for fear of being viewed as wrong. In a world full of the perception of perfection, to be honest, and say, *"I am imperfect,"* is defeating. Still, we all have a sense of imperfection because we all know we have fallen short. Therefore, to project being perfect into our thinking, many think we must act as though we have never done anything negative.

The biggest problem with this line of thinking is this: Someone can feel or think they are the ones performing God's will, and it is not the manifestation of His Spirit inside of them doing so. Therefore, when the devil reminds them of their wrong, the sense of perfection is automatically lost. This is the "break one" law; we have broken the law period standpoint. Therefore, we are forever tainted. When evaluating itself, the carnal mindset thinks of the lifetime of our flesh, not the instantaneous mindset and spirit we are in.

The carnal mind identifies with the flesh, our bodies. Most people spend large portions of their lives thinking of themselves from the fleshly perspective. This means that a lot of people go through life thinking, acting, and choosing from the perspective of what they have experienced, as opposed to what they know in their spirit. They allow their flesh to dictate to the Spirit, as opposed to having the Spirit dictate to the flesh. All the knowledge and understanding that have come into our lives can never trump the knowledge and understanding of the Holy Spirit inside us. The fact that God makes the sun to shine and the rain to rain, over the just and the unjust alike, should allow everyone to see, God treats no one differently, even though people acknowledge, honor, respect, and reverence God differently. Until we start to accept these kinds of simple truths, we will not truly be ready to work on ourselves. How can we work on ourselves if we refuse to identify who we truly are?

The fact that God makes the sun shine and the rain to rain, over the just and the unjust alike, should allow everyone to see, God treats no one differently, even though people acknowledge, honor, respect, and reverence God differently.

Our self-identification happens in times of crisis and tragedy. We realize how much we've messed up a certain situation, or how we could have handled something differently or better. We don't usually fully accept and admit what bad decision-makers we are. Why? Because we quickly reinforce the bad decisions we have made, with good ones.

We praise ourselves for all the accomplishments and successes we have had. We think of all our strong traits, so they can counteract and over compensate for the bad ones. We think of all the gains we have made in other areas of life, so we can have and keep an overall good feeling about ourselves.

This type of thinking will always allow "mediocre" to appear "good enough." We never want to fully admit to ourselves that perfection is attainable. If we admit that perfection is attainable, the next question we must ask ourselves is: Then why haven't we achieved it?

These types of admissions are the very reasons why most people will never look themselves fully in the mirror in order to see their true reflection. They look in the mirror, and their images are distorted toward positive untruths.

The truth we must acknowledge is, God is God alone. The Bible depicts God as all-knowing; nothing can be added nor taken away from His truth, knowledge, and understanding. Everything good in life comes from Him. Everything bad in life comes from the devil. The devil cannot do anything God doesn't allow him to do. The devil wants to be on God's level, as opposed to following in His footsteps. Lucifer wanted humans to have understanding and wanted us to become equal to God. He believed that his thinking could be superior to God's. He leaned on his own understanding over God's. These are the truths we must admit, so we can see our true bondage to limited knowledge and understanding.

When we operate on the same grounds from which Lucifer was cast down to Earth, we must understand our flesh, and therefore our connection to the same limited understanding. Once we choose to think and operate from our own understanding, we automatically cut ourselves off from God's, but God is trying to give us what we are searching for. His rights and wrongs are already given to us.

It is up to us to understand that we can operate from the same standpoint of limited knowledge and understanding as Lucifer does, or we can choose to follow God. Our fleshly desire is linked to the devil, including the mindset we develop outside of God. We then come to the real root of the situation: Our thinking.

Our thinking is what is evil, and it is from our foolish ways that God is trying to save us from. Our thinking is at the core of everything we stand for and believe. However, our own thinking, understanding, and knowledge are forever flawed, and we are easily swayed and misled. The pride in our thinking makes us too stubborn to accept change. Being too stubborn to accept change makes us all susceptible to being foolish. We must reach the conclusion that our own thinking leads to folly.

God alone is perfect. Unless we join Him in perfection, via listening to His Spirit, we will forever be flawed, foolish, and lukewarm. We must accept that we are the ones who fall short continually; we constantly make the same mistakes. We must come to accept, no matter how much we want to change ourselves, we always will fall short. We will always revert to backsliding, thinking perfection isn't a possibility, let alone ever trying to achieve and maintain it.

This is when the carnal mind completely reveals itself. The carnal mind brings to the forefront of our mind, everything except what God has for us to do. We are the ones who think we can outsmart Him, just like Lucifer thought. We try to cheat the system, as opposed to operating inside of it. We are the disobedience we refuse to make right. The flesh is forever in sin because of its linkage to carnality. Our carnality is what makes us sinful.

Our carnality is not subject to God's will. We must choose to give it up, once we realize what it is and what it represents. We are the ones who constantly argue with God, as opposed to simply listening to Him. We have been taught erroneously, and that is why we aren't able to identify His Spirit. The fear of God should translate to the fear of the Holy Spirit. To not listen to the Holy Spirit is to knowingly set ourselves up for downfalls. Every time we go against what we know to be entirely right, we set ourselves up for failure.

Every time we don't do what is right, we allow the devil to use our memory against us. Every time we choose to go our own way, we choose to go against what God's Spirit is instructing us to do. We oftentimes run from the truth, scared and fearful to go against the grain. Our carnality pretends for others, and we go along, acting as though it has achieved perfection on its own accord. In our carnality, we constantly try to outsmart others' judgments and opinions, as opposed to learning from our carnality-based mistakes.

The outsmarting we attempt only applies to us as individuals, and it is nothing more than our vanity, pride, and ego at play and on display. All the vanity, ego, and pride we possess are just our foolishness being displayed to others. Once we accept that anything outside of the Spirit is carnality, we can start the process of learning to see ourselves for who we truly are. Then, throughout life, we can recognize and admit to all the erroneous (sinful) mindsets we have taken on.

We can begin to realize that we can be anything and everything under the sun, if we choose to be. We realize, when we are operating as ourselves, we always fall for some scheme the devil has to offer. We can reach the conclusion, as much as our mother, father, brother, sister, wife/husband, children, extended family, and friends have tried to help us become good, even our own attempts have fallen short of what we need to do.

Once we admit to ourselves, we are no more than sinners, we can finally see why we need to be and should be saved from ourselves. We are the carnal mind, linked to the devil. Therefore, we are forever linked to flawed thinking, inferior knowledge, mediocre understanding, and worthless wisdom. There is nothing we can do, nor anything we can try on our own accord, which can defeat this simple fact. We as individuals are linked to the devil and flesh; we are carnal and carnally minded; we are enmity against God. Our thinking is the issue and the problem we must get rid of. We are all sinners!

Once we admit to ourselves, we are no more than sinners, we can finally see why we need to be and should be saved from ourselves.

The Carnal Mind

My bills were easily paid with the extra money from being in Afghanistan. My bank account was sitting nice and pretty, and I was in the best shape of my life. Life should have been great, right? However, I had to admit that my joy was far from "complete." I could have had all the happiness in the world, then a negative situation would present itself, and I would fall prey to frustration, bitterness, judgment, and at times, anger.

YOU DON'T LISTEN.

I am listening! I apply everything you tell me to, and the issues of life are still the issues of life.

DO YOU HONESTLY THINK YOU LISTEN AND OBEY?

There wasn't a need for any rebuttal; I knew I didn't truly listen and obey. Each day, I tried my hardest to achieve this perfection I knew existed. I just couldn't maintain it. I started to think back on life and all the times I chose to listen to myself, instead of listening to what I knew was the ultimate truth. Through all the whippings I'd gotten as a kid, all the tough spots and rough patches I hit from being hard-headed and stubborn as an adult, I knew the Holy Spirit had given me advice and instruction. I had to admit. I just didn't take nor accept any of it. The song, *Isn't It Ironic* (Ballard, G. & Morrissette, A. M. 1996) became extra clear to me.

I began to understand and own up to all the things that had sent me on a tangent in life; I was responsible for all of them. I was the one constantly acting as though I could outsmart God. In my personal life, I didn't know the proper way to instruct and lead my wife. My sons were constantly a battle in my mind. I struggled between providing for them and being so far away from them. I knew no amount of material things could trump love. I knew that all there was to life was love. However, as the saying goes, "love doesn't pay the bills."

WITH LOVE, YOU HAVE NO BILLS.

Have no bills? I know it is possible, but how do I get others to realize that?

I started becoming an example of love, but I still had no clue how deeply and how manipulative the devil's schemes could truly go. As time went on, my walk became narrower and straighter. I began to chase the fruits of the Holy Spirit. On some bad days, negative thinking would slip in, but I knew the fruits of the Spirit were love, joy, peace, long-suffering, gentleness, goodness, faith, meekness, and temperance. Consistently maintaining that state of mind, however, always had a way of escaping me. The light finally came on.

YOU'RE JUST REALIZING THAT YOU CAN'T DO IT ON YOUR OWN?

Yeah. Yeah. I know, I should have known, only You can give me these things. It isn't for me to go out and try to pursue them. It is for me to receive and accept them from You.

I remembered a verse I had read.

YOU STILL TRYING TO TAKE CREDIT, HUH?

Ok!

The Holy Spirit pointed me to scripture I had skimmed across a few days earlier.

Hebrews 5:8-9;

"Though he were a Son, yet learned he obedience by the things which he suffered; And being made perfect, he became the author of eternal salvation unto all them that obey him."

Hold on.

YES, RYAN.

You mean to tell me...

YES, RYAN.

Well, why doesn't anyone explain or present this information?

THEY HAVEN'T BEEN CHOSEN.

Haven't been chosen? Where do I go with that information?

JUST KEEP WALKING!

I guess I have to stop trying to put the milk before the cow. Are we, as humans, really that bad? Can we truly identify ourselves as negative? Why would we ever identify ourselves to be something other than good?

We work our entire lives to build up a good reputation and credibility. Therefore, we never want to accept that we are inherently bad as individuals. As extreme as everything we've been taught has been, no one wants to admit to extremes of being bad. By thinking of the extremes of anything, to be in the middle of that extreme makes you not be the extreme. The carnal mind keeps alive the idea that we can be good on our own accord.

Due to the compare-and-contrast society we live in, no one accepts negativity as a trait we carry along with us. We never want to admit to ourselves we are negative, especially if there is a possibility someone else is truly positive. No one admits completely to all the knowledge and understanding they are lacking. Everyone wants to feel superior in some way, overlooking what being equal to others brings.

All these self-identity issues lead to a lot of confusion in our minds, and therefore our behavior as well. We want to overlook our wrongs so badly; we never find a way to fully release our past sins. Likewise, we are never fully able to forgive others. By constantly bringing up our past sins, we naturally keep a record of others' wrongs, too. We are ready and always prepared to defend our pride, ego, and vanity, so providing facts and evidence of others' past wrongs becomes, "I just told the truth."

We are the judgmental "negative Nancy" who is waiting to rob another of their joy. We are the ones who are steadily asking and saying, "You sure? You think you can do all that? Are you sure you want to do all that work? If that were me, I would never do it." We, as individuals, are the ones who place fear and doubt into others. We have no place evaluating another's life. On our own accord, we are just as foolish and unwise as anyone else.

When evaluating others' lives, we make statements like, "I don't understand why he/she is so happy. He/she should be stressed and worried about this. I don't know why he/she put up with it. He/she is stupid and should give up." Once we are done with our judging and evaluating, however, we are all quick to say, "I don't know how they do it."

At the root of all these mindsets, or ways of thinking, are judgment and evaluation. Only then can we see the error of our ways. Judging and evaluating others automatically puts us into the wilderness. It is there that we understand that a carnal mind is a mind in the wilderness. A carnal mind is void of the ability to distinguish and truly define its rights from its wrongs, and the extremes thereof, because it is reprobate (Romans Chapter 1). Once we become curious, we automatically send our minds on a tangent. Any tangent we go on in life is never complete, until it returns to the starting point.

The tangents of life use the same energy meant for our true purpose. Therefore, we must return from any tangent of life we are on, if we want to use all our energy and power for our true purpose. Stripping away the time and energy powering a tangent of life is the only way it can die. In truth, however, nothing wants to die. If nothing wants to die, the only way to return to zero from the starting point is to go the full 360 degrees.

We must go through the entire process to understand why we should have never gone on that tangent of life in the first place. We must return our energy to the main source; we must be willing to give ourselves over to the Holy Spirit inside of us.

All the tangents in our minds deplete the energy that the Holy Spirit could be using. Until we accept this simple truth, we will not recognize that any energy we use to wander and wonder, is the energy we are not using to make a true difference in our lives and in the world. The wilderness leaves us in a zombie-like state, wandering and wondering through life with no sense of true purpose or direction.

The wilderness leaves us in a zombie-like state, wandering and wondering through life with no sense of true purpose or direction.

Many people spend their entire lives in a state of wonder . Wondering how they got to where they are. Some numb themselves from thinking of the what-ifs and the possibilities of life, only to allow themselves to continue suffering within the daily grind. Some trick themselves into looking down on others; they do this to feel they have it better than others. What they never do is look up to see the number of people who have it better than them.

We have all been taught to try and balance our ego, as opposed to getting rid of it, and everything it stands for. All these tangents amount to distractions, which ultimately limit us from devoting the proper energy into the things that matter. The more tangents we create, the further and deeper into the wilderness we go. The more we think we can conquer life and overcome tangents on our own, the deeper into the wilderness and further on a tangent of life we go.

The key to life is eliminating the tangents by recognizing them as disobedience to the Holy Spirit. Look at all the meaningful moments and decisions we have made in our lives. We will see every time we did not follow after God; we led ourselves into destruction. We start to understand how we bring negativity into our lives. It isn't like we always go looking for it. We must admit, however we sometimes go headfirst into some things, already knowing we are dead wrong. Either way, we still must be willing to admit the truth when it is brought to our attention.

We must identify when we are being beyond reproach. We must identify when we are scorning those who are only there trying to help us. We all must strive to continuously operate inside the borderlines of wisdom, which is to thank and love all the more those who take the time, energy, and effort to correct us.

Correction should be a welcomed thing, as opposed to something to be frowned upon. Nothing is wrong with being and getting corrected. Everything is wrong with staying wrong, once we are corrected. Until we start to truly look for the proper correction, we cannot be perfected. We cannot be fully repented to the Holy Spirit until we want our thoughts, decisions, actions, and deeds reproved by Him. We all know the Holy Spirit is perfect. The question we all ask should be: How can we become perfect, as Our Father in Heaven is perfect when we are being drawn to our salvation?

When we start to strive for our salvation, we must come to grips with certain truths. We know we are saved, but what does that mean? If we are saved, why do our decisions even matter? We can just do what we want anyway, right? All these thoughts enter our minds as we transition from our carnal minds because they are at odds with the Holy Spirit.

The carnal mind is not subject to the Holy Spirit's control. It is free of the Holy Spirit's guidance. The carnal mind looks at the Holy Spirit's guidance as an option, opinion, or suggestion but not as a direct order from God. The carnal mind looks at the Holy Spirit inside of us as part of ourselves. By us being taught that we have a conscience, we separated ourselves from God. We pray to God on one hand, then argue with the Holy Spirit on the other. We cannot identify the Trinity because we can't accept the true Trinity. We can't get past the physical in order to step into the Spiritual. The carnal mind refuses to die because everything it knows must die with it; this means that we never want to become fully saved because we don't want to die to ourselves (our own thinking) in the process.

The carnal mind wants to exist. Therefore, to identify something that goes against it takes a lot of humility. For us to get to the point of hating ourselves takes a lot of admission.

- We have to admit that we are disobedient.
- We have to admit that we can do better.
- We have to admit that we should slow down to be able to think correctly.
- We must admit our faults and shortcomings.
- We have to admit that every time we lean on our own understanding, and overthink, the energy we use worrying and thinking on our own accord is pointless and useless.
- We must admit that we don't have to stress.
- We must admit that we don't have to worry.
- We must admit that we need to exercise and be healthy.
- We have to admit that we should be eating better.
- We have to admit that we know we are supposed to be active in our community and others' lives.
- We have to admit that we should have better control over our actions.
- We must admit that the best version of ourselves exists before we can believe in it, let alone achieve it.
- The carnal mind (our thinking) is full of doubt and fear.
- The carnal mind learns to hide doubt and fear, by labeling it as being realistic and/or safe. Its two biggest allies and/or choice of weapons to use against us are the past and the future.
- The carnal mind must learn to slow down to the moment; only then can it slow down enough to begin to understand.
- The carnal mind must learn humility, patience, how to forgive, how to not be boastful, and how to remain and stay positive.
- The carnal mind has to learn how to not let its peace be disturbed, and how to operate beyond its capabilities.
- The carnal mind, after trying so hard, must understand that it will never be enough.
- The carnal mind must admit that it can easily be defeated by life.
- The carnal mind must further understand that it is under the devil's control and manipulation.

Once we accept that having a carnal mind means we are under the devil's control, we can finally understand the severity of getting rid of our carnal mind (our own thinking)!

Our carnal minds are within our nature. We naturally become curious on our own, and once we accept, we are in the wilderness of our thinking. We can finally accept the path to get out of that wilderness. The exit out of the wilderness appears when we finally come 360o, with and within ourselves, and return to zero. Only then can we be led by the Holy Spirit without our own interference. We have to stop wondering on our own. We must understand and accept, to be in the wilderness means, we must be in our flesh. We have to abandon our flesh in order to be freed from our carnality. The carnal mind is anything outside of allowing the Holy Spirit to flow through us.

The results of being led by and walking in the Spirit are clearly defined. We must accept that we bring our carnal mind (our thinking) to the table. It is only God who can give us the one and only true spiritual mind to be had. The walk through the wilderness still works together for our good, because it allows us to understand and accept the truth. We cannot add nor take away from God; we accept that God alone is perfect. By this acceptance and admission, we can then tune into the Holy Spirit. It exists. Until we admit that perfection exists, we can never put away the things that keep us apart from the perfection within the Holy Spirit.

A carnal mind is any mindset outside of the Holy Spirit. If we have to ask, *what would Jesus do?*, we aren't operating inside the Holy Spirit. If we were, there would be no reason to have to ask. We would just do what we know to be right. Therefore, we must accept and admit when we are being carnal. To admit that we are carnal is the same as admitting that we are sinners. Before we can see that there is more to tap into inside ourselves, where the Holy Spirit seeks to dwell, we have to admit that there is more to life than operating as sinners.

The Holy Spirit is lost as a whisper inside a sinner's mind. Too many other thoughts and scenarios are also running through the minds of carnal individuals. We must calm down and transition into the mindset that gives us the peace that passes all understanding. Love in its entirety is the thing our carnal mind refuses to accept. If our actions aren't full of love, then we must accept and understand that we still have some perfecting to accomplish. The refinement process is only as long as we make it. We must willingly give up our carnal mind in order to accept a Spiritual one, a Spirit-filled one.

The Holy Spirit is lost as a whisper inside a sinner's mind.

Step One in the salvation process is admitting that we are sinners with a carnal mind. The next step is separating the carnal mind from the Holy Spirit. Once we begin identifying the things of God, everything it takes to have a spiritual mind is revealed. The refinement process is when we begin getting to know what we are still bringing to the table, even in our pursuit of doing and wanting to be good. The refinement stage reveals all the strongholds we have left in our minds that we refuse to release. These include all thoughts and thinking that prevent us from evolving into the spiritual beings that we are.

The carnal mind is of the devil. It tries to stay in us, even when we think it is gone. It makes us think we can't live without it, because we automatically think of the carnal mind as ourselves, hence the reason we must die to self in order to operate and live in the Spirit. In conclusion, the carnal mind must accept that our returning to zero is the only way to achieve a change of 360o. It is only vanity and pride that want to fill up our egos in the belief that we can achieve perfection on our own, and of our own accord. Each prodigal son and daughter must return home, not look to make a new one elsewhere.

The Transition

After spending the last year and a couple of months in the deserts of Afghanistan, I was able to love and show love to everyone with whom I came in contact. I finally got to the point where a woman's looks did not register with my lust, as well. I learned the lesson of giving others the opportunity to grow, because God had given me the ability to do so. I learned to stop being judgmental, because the result of judging others is negativity. I realized that I had been judging a person first, to feel any negative emotion or thought. Therefore, to stay inside of God's will, I realized that I couldn't judge others. Judging automatically reveals and presents the negatives of life.

I was finally at a point where the gist of performing God's will had become uplifting. I began to encourage others in their journeys. I had finally arrived.

OR SO YOU THOUGHT.

We're not there yet.

After returning to the states, life hit me hard. Having to balance the fast-pacedness of being back stateside was too much. I succumbed. All the preparation I had done while in the desert was slowly replaced with the daily grind of life. I started to look outward, instead of inward. The constant flow of negative energy quickly depleted the positive energy I thought I possessed. I wondered if it was even worth it. My carnality was back in an instant, but I didn't know it. It had been there the entire time, just waiting for me to lower my guard. My carnality allowed me to think

I could do it on my own accord and still live a life pleasing to God. My carnality played dead and slowly convinced me that it was killed, which meant that I did not need the effort of killing it daily.

I thought I had arrived, but I failed to take into account my not dying daily. Slowly, as the days without renewing my mind began to pile on, the old Ryan's thinking had eased its way back into my mind. I then realized how sneaky my carnal self could be. He had reappeared with no notice or announcement. I had been operating as myself, still being myself, while thinking I was living in the Spirit. I had to soul-search again. Only then did I realize how important it was, while doing well, to remember on my own accord, I am just a sinner. Once life starts going well, it is hard to remain focused on the reality that you are still the evil in the equation. The feeling of being on top of life can begin to stroke your ego in different ways, ways you are not prepared for because you never experienced that type of success.

By this point, I owned two houses. I was on my way, living the American dream. I was renting out a house in Houston while living in a house on 35 acres of land in Colorado, which was just transitioning into legal marijuana. You can probably guess what happened next. I figured it would be unwise of me not to tap into the market.

I KEPT TELLING YOU IT WASN'T THE WAY, RYAN.

I figured it would be a startup seed for all the endeavors that were placed on my heart to carry out. I figured it would be a controversial issue for some, but no one could deny the benefit it could be in the future. As time went on, I had both outdoor and indoor gardens. I could look out and see the start of what things were to become.

RYAN, DO YOU REALLY WANT TO BE INVOLVED IN THIS?

WHAT WILL MY PEOPLE THINK OF THIS?

They should be happy I won't be asking them for tithes every five seconds.

RYAN!

I'm saying, this is a good opportunity. Why pass it up? I am doing my best to fulfill all the things You place on my heart. They should cut me a break and have understanding. I don't see anyone else helping!

The transition from our thinking to God's thinking can be a tricky one. We have to willingly and steadily be in the Holy Spirit. This can be a very trying and tiring process for most of us. We can easily feel like we are giving our all but to no avail. We can easily continue to look at all the *why even try* factors of life. It isn't until we give our best effort at becoming tuned to the Holy Spirit that the process can truly start. Everyone must find out the same truth: we won't be able to do it. We will continue to spend time trying to fit a square peg through a round hole. We have to identify all the ways of the carnal mind, in order to truly get rid of it. A lot of people call it hitting rock bottom.

A lot of us choose to remain lukewarm; we are unwilling to experience an extreme of bad and are therefore too cautious to allow ourselves to see or recognize the fullness of our wrongs and wrongdoings. Therefore, a *"here a little, there a little"* approach is how we apply the Holy Spirit into our lives. This stage of life can take years to go through, and countless amounts of trials and tribulations. We want to identify with the good acts we have done and detach ourselves from the bad ones. However, this stage of life reminds us of being sinners. The reminder, we are still yet sinners can easily defeat the average individual and allow them to return to the version of themselves they know most, the carnal mind (their own thinking). The cycle is never broken or completed, due to the *"here a little, there a little"* approach.

Tackling being lukewarm head-on has to be done in truth. We have to realize we only did all the good we have done because of the Holy Spirit, plus all of the bad we did, the second we abandoned the Holy Spirit.

- All things are lawful for me, but all things are not expedient.
- All things are lawful for me, but all things edify not. 1 Corinthians 10:23.

These two statements make the transition into operating inside the Holy Spirit difficult for some of us to understand. Once we understand the Holy Spirit, we can never believe that God would be slow or not be uplifting. Therefore, why would we, as vessels to His Spirit, perform in such an underachieving way, if we have received the Holy Spirit? The transition into the Holy Spirit can be very confusing, until we admit what the Holy Spirit is. A lot of times, we feel we have made it into the Holy Spirit when we are still operating as ourselves, and therefore, carnally. No one seems bold enough to say, it is only the Holy Spirit that can save us.

The Holy Spirit inside of us is the same as the Holy Spirit inside of Jesus. His flesh was just a vessel. Once we understand that Jesus' flesh was a vessel, we can then understand that we are all vessels. Once we accept that we are vessels too, we can then understand and accept. We are supposed to be vessels and temples to house Our Father, as well.

RYAN, TELL THEM AGAIN!

He is the Father of all, the Creator. Jesus is our Savior by giving us an example of how to fulfill Our Father's will for our lives.

I AM THE GOD OF ALL FLESH.

I am getting there.

We all must return to the first promise. We all are on the threshing floor, waiting and wanting to be grafted back into the tree that produces good fruit. Jesus produced much fruit. He not only allowed Our Father to use Him, but He also always projected Our Father's Spirit to the world. He humbly chose to serve, as opposed to telling everyone to worship Him. Most carnal people want a piece of Our Father's glory, as opposed to giving Him all the glory and honor. The limelight on our lives from Our Father's Spirit can easily make some of us backslide into restoring our pride, vanity, and ego.

One of the biggest things to accept about Our Father's Spirit is it isn't self-seeking. For that reason alone, we all must accept we are outside of Our

Father's will, when we become self-seeking. Most of us want to think, we are the ones who are accepting the Spirit, so we can feel worthy of some of the praise. If we stop trying to take credit for the good things in life, we stop feeling so beat up, when the bad things come around. Furthermore, by wanting to stroke own egos, we add to the bad things of life. Our Father can give us this well-oiled machine, where everything is going perfectly at any moment in our lives. We will, in turn, want to put our personal touches on our lives, causing more suffering, turmoil, and pain. The second we make life about ourselves; it is easy to evaluate it along these terms: Is my life making me happy? This question sounds innocent at first glance. However, it confirms that we have a self-seeking spirit.

The only way to escape this mindset is to start the process of looking outward instead of inward when it comes to spreading love and positivity, and inward instead of outward when it comes to judgment and trying to find negativity. When we begin to look outward, we notice the struggle of those around us as well. The same battles we are facing, our brothers and sisters around the world are facing. We oftentimes try to look for the same situation to happen the same exact way. Therefore, we always overlook the same exact problem, when it is handed to us differently. The problem with life is the devil, and his attempts at robbing us of our joy. We want to believe that the devil would be hard to identify with and relate to, without understanding that we have been riding with the devil our entire lives and trying to break free. The carnal mind is our natural thinking. The carnal mind is our own knowledge and understanding. The carnal mind always tries to paint itself as wise when it is the source of all foolishness. When we stop overlooking our flaws and look inward towards our negativity, we can finally get to work on ourselves.

The carnal mind always tries to paint itself as wise when it is the source of all foolishness.

When we start the process of spreading love towards others, we realize that it is always demanded of us. We then begin to question how it is even possible, given everything we must deal with in life. We start the process of accepting that we must get rid of our negativity, and the things that make us negative, to always project love and positivity onto our brothers and sisters. We begin to struggle with giving love to those who wronged us. We start to wonder how we can do these things and not feel like others are taking advantage of us. We start to relate and identify with others' feelings and emotions behind their pain and hurt. We can easily fall back into a *why do we even try* mentality and end the process of becoming spiritual. We start to see how evil others can be. We start to admit how evil we are. We start to see ourselves for the true disobedient individuals we are.

We continue to try to fight the good fight. However, with every two steps in the right direction, we feel like ten steps just pulled us back in the opposite direction. In the transitioning process, the key to keep moving forward is to remain humble, and to realize, we already know we are the ones who will bring the bad to the table. The challenge of it all is to understand immediately, when we ourselves are present in our thoughts, it automatically means we are wandering in the wilderness. Our Father has a neat file cabinet of lessons learned and joyful memories stored in our minds. We are the ones who erroneously interpret that to mean failures and what life could, should, or would be like if this or that hadn't happened. Some of us can't realize how good we've got it, because we have experienced too many high points in life for our own good. We finally start to see that the true battle is over us, and it is between our carnality (the devil) and Holy Spirit.

The battle lies in our decision-making. It is in who and what we allow to influence our decisions. When we all sit back and take an objective point of view, we all recognize true right from real wrong. If we were all in charge of an avatar on a computer or a video game, we would all choose to do what is best to build up our character and beat the game. It wouldn't matter what suffering our avatar might feel towards the necessary training, proper eating, and exercise. Whatever he, she, or it has to learn to defeat the game would have to be done. We wouldn't stop until we had a fully functional avatar/character that could go on and not only face whatever game it is we are playing but excel at it and defeat it too.

Right from wrong is clear and cut and dry. It is those feelings and emotions of ours, in response to what is right and wrong, that we must overcome. Our response to right and wrong has to change. One of the most crucial facts a carnal mind must accept is this: Only change is true repentance. Too often, we have been taught and accepted as the truth, that just saying, "I am sorry" means something. It is something that was invented to appease a person's ears. Those are some words that are soothing to others' egos, pride, and feelings. The thought process of, "I can now perform the action Our Father commanded of us, because someone was willing to apologize," has to be debunked.

The question we really must answer is: For whom did we perform that act of forgiveness? The question of whose reward we are seeking comes to the forefront of our thinking; we realize the error in our ways. "I am sorry" is just a way to remain cordial and appease a situation. If a person sins against us, pull them to the side, explain our cause, and if he or she repents, forgive. Why? Isn't that exactly how Our Father deals with us? He brings things to the forefront of our minds. If we take heed and change our thinking, it is like what we thought of never entered our minds in the first place. If we don't take heed, life has a way of making us wish we had. This is all part of Our Father's process.

Even in our carnality, we realize why we should be spiritual. The battle is to understand; we have no reason to ever trust in our own thinking. Every time we show up in our thoughts, we need to be able to recognize we bring the devil with us. As much as we don't want to do so, due to our flesh, we automatically do so. Our pride must be lowered for us to accept that our own thinking shouldn't exist.

Once we accept who we have defined ourselves to be is our pride, we can start to tap into the mindset. We can be anything. When we realize we can be anything, we are finally ready to fine-tune who we are. Once we begin to fine-tune the process of who and what we should be, we realize that nothing is better than being a vessel for Our Father. Not only must we *want* to give love at all times cheerfully, but we must also give love at all times. We must leave our carnality behind, in order to live in our salvation. Our Father's Spirit is grace and mercy. Grace and mercy combined are unconditional love. Unconditional love is the source of charity. Without charity, we are all nothing.

Once we begin to fine-tune the process of who and what we should be, we realize that nothing is better than being a vessel for Our Father.

Grace and Mercy

I can't believe this! All I ever try to do is help. Why am I getting screwed over? What am I going to do now?

I TOLD YOU THIS WASN'T THE WAY.

You never told me what the way was, either. I wanted this to be the seed money to do Your will.

YOU ALWAYS HAVE TO GO BIG AND NOT SMALL.

What is the purpose of going small, if You are backing me? Why wouldn't I put my all into You and try to make the biggest impact possible? I kept going because of my faith in You and nothing else.

YOU WERE BLINDED BY GAIN.

Whatever!

THIS STARTED AS YOUR DREAM HOUSE. YOU ARE ALREADY THINKING OF BUILDING ANOTHER. YOU PROMISED TO START SPREADING THE GOSPEL. YOU HAVE PUT ALL YOUR MONEY, ATTENTION, FOCUS, AND ENERGY INTO MARIJUANA GROWING.

I always try to put people on. I always try to get people's attention for you.

RYAN? WE BOTH KNOW YOUR TRUE CAPABILITIES.

I can't believe this is happening. Everything was going so well. I could just kill 'em. I can't understand how people who know they are soft, try to be so hard. Dealing with the lost can be so difficult at times. None of the "tough guys" I have ever met was really tough. I wish I would have…

RYAN, WHY? WHAT IS ALL THIS GOING TO DO? YOU'RE NOT ABOUT TO KILL ANYONE. YOU KNOW YOU STILL WISH THEM THE BEST. WHY DON'T YOU UNDERSTAND YOU HAVE TO APPLY THE SAME THINGS TO OTHERS AS I DO TO YOU?

Man, I worked to attain all of this!

PLEASE, YOU KNOW I GAVE YOU ALL OF THIS.

You know what? (laughing hysterically at this moment in my mind) You are right.

I put myself into this situation. I didn't stay in tune with the Spirit. All the decisions I made came flooding into the memories of my mind. All the decisions that led me to this point, where I strayed from what the Holy Spirit was telling me to do, showed themselves at once. I couldn't do anything but forgive others.

You see, someone called the police. The police came. The police saw some cans they believed weren't supposed to be there. Next thing you know, SWAT is at my door. *SWAT at my door?*

Why in the hell is SWAT even here?

I TOLD YOU THIS WASN'T THE WAY. THE COMPANY YOU KEEP IS DETERMINED BY THE CHOICES YOU MAKE.

Now is not the time for a lesson. I am potentially about to be arrested.

WHAT DID YOU DO WRONG?

Nothing.

WELL, WHY ARE YOU FREAKING OUT?

These guns, these handcuffs, all these people at my house!

Everything I worked for, gone in the blink of an eye. All the money I invested, went in the same blink of an eye. Anger was there, waiting for me to take the bait and act like a plum fool.

REMEMBER THE WARNING I GAVE YOU, OF SPEAKING INTO EXISTENCE, YOU ARE GOING TO COST ME A QUARTER-MILLION DOLLARS?

At the time I said it, I was raging with anger. But...

WHAT IS YOUR PRICE ON LOVE?

It was silent but deadly to everything else going on in my mind. It silenced every feeling and emotion I was experiencing. I realized that it was all destined. I realized that everything works together for our good. I have never had a true setback in life. Everything I have acquired has always been better. I understood I could bestow one of the greatest lessons of life on two individuals, or I could be like everyone else. I chose for Our Father to be able to use me as a lesson in the future in both parties' lives. Once they mature in life, I hope the Holy Spirit will be able to reveal to them that it was all love and a big life lesson to all involved. I realized then, grace and mercy are the only true steppingstones to unconditional love. If we claim to believe in Our Father, we must live by grace and mercy. I can never fall victim to thinking someone doesn't deserve grace and mercy.

Grace and mercy are glorified and rightfully so. Grace and mercy are our affirmations that Our Father loves us. It is how we can feel His love, even when we know we are unworthy. Grace and mercy are the reasons we love

God so much. Grace and mercy are the sources of our connection to Him. We understand and know, without grace and mercy, we are unworthy of His love and protection. Grace and mercy are what keep us going. When we truly know that we messed up big time, to the point we should not be able to move forward, these two actions are the reasons we all know and understand that God's love for us is unconditional. Grace and mercy, though, are just a thoroughfare to favor. Understanding the complicity of it all is key for understanding how we should be. With all thy getting, get understanding, because it requires understanding to apply the knowledge we receive in life as wisdom.

With all thy getting, get understanding, because it requires understanding to apply the knowledge we receive in life as wisdom.

Grace and mercy are open doors that allow us to feel as though we can come and go. To say that this is a lie or not the truth, would be us refusing to admit to ourselves who we truly are. Grace and mercy can be very confusing to some. If God loves us, why does anything we do matter? If God loves us more than our earthly fathers love us, why should we ever look past grace and mercy? A sinner who gets grace and mercy should smile for receiving it. A spiritual person smiles because of giving it; a spiritual person receives and understands favor. Therefore, a spiritual person also recognizes grace and mercy simply as a gateway to favor. Grace and mercy are how we should all interact with each other.

Favor is reserved for those who are in the Spirit. We do this all the time without realizing it. Grace and mercy are how and why we give an old friend the benefit of the doubt in getting him or her a job. Favor would be us recommending an old friend for a job, without him or her even knowing it. Those who have shown and given us love throughout our lives, stand out in our memory. The second we can repay the favor, we do.

We need to humble ourselves to understand, it is not our will to be done, but Our Father's. No one can come into our lives deserving of anything. Anyone we evaluate will always fall short of the glory of God, meaning no man will ever be perfect. Neither will we achieve perfection on our own accord. We are so busy not applying grace and mercy on ourselves, we can never see past the past. The past is something that can never be understood without grace and mercy. If we always look at ourselves from a fleshly perspective, our past will forever be attached to us. As long as our past is attached to us, our past sins are too. Our memories from the record of our wrongs never allow us to operate as complete or whole.

Grace and mercy are just the starting process of getting us headed towards Our Father. This process allows us to understand. It is possible to get there. It helps us feel empowered and encouraged. When we honestly know, we are trying to do our best in life, we automatically feel connected to Our Father. When we know we are following after what is right, we automatically know that Our Father is present in our midst. With that being said, we all need to realize that everything goes both ways. In life, we have to give grace and mercy to everyone we meet.

Those who need it should get it freely and receive it in abundance. We are all commanded to love as our Savior loved. We all have to bear our own cross in order to cross over into the Spiritual mindset. Grace and mercy are how we are allowed to see ourselves for who we are, and to be able to repent. Grace and mercy are how we build towards becoming perfected, even when we aren't operating as such.

Grace and mercy are how we are allowed to see ourselves for who we are, and to be able to repent.

We must apply these same principles to others, as we apply them to ourselves. We have to apply them to others in order for us to feel comfortable applying them to ourselves. Grace and mercy are how we start to build ourselves up in the Spirit. Just because we are entitled to grace and mercy doesn't mean we can assume that we possess the Holy Spirit.

Grace and mercy are our access to the Holy Spirit. Once we are in the midst of Our Father, we have to learn how to operate there, and understand and accept, we can't operate just any kind of way in Our Father's presence. We want to think of Our Father's presence as unique and rare. However, our Father wants to be in the midst of all of our thoughts. We now can see how God is there for the just and unjust. Meaning, there is no difference. The unjust don't apply the same truths as the just. The just ones realize listening to the Holy Spirit is the only way to remain just. The unjust think that the baseline of right is the beginning stage of what they should or shouldn't do, based on the expectations of man and their emotions and feelings.

Someone ready to get past grace and mercy is ready to surpass doing the minimum in life. The minimum in life seems easy to establish and maintain. However, to surpass the minimum in life seems like a daunting task. In work, life, relationships, education, stewardship, and anything else dealing in right and wrong, we must look to show ourselves approved by Our Father, not by man. Our Father wants more than our minimum. He wants our all.

We want to make it seem like Our Father's judgment is less than man's. Not understanding, Our Father's judgment far surpasses that of man's. With our deeds on Earth, we can easily be fooled into thinking we are good. Our Father, on the other hand, comes out and says our deeds are like filthy rags unto Him. So consumed by the thoughts and judgment of others, we fail to see the truth from Our Father. He has already declared every man's heart is in His hands and under His control.

Therefore, there is nothing man can do that Our Father does not allow him to. We must stop trying to act as though we, as individuals, are more than anything but filthy rags. All sinners are filthy rags. All human beings are filthy rags. Everyone in life is filthy. This had to be done and played out so all of us would be in need of grace and mercy. No one man can be over another. No one can be esteemed over the other. All of us have fallen short. However, all of us can easily be washed clean, if we have enough patience and humility to be washed clean. Grace and mercy are there for the transitioning. They are not the final product.

Grace and mercy are there for the backslider and sinner. Our lives should amount to more than being a sinner and a backslider. Grace and mercy should be something we give, not receive, for to receive, we must have escaped favor. The question then becomes: What is so special about favor, compared to grace and mercy? Isn't love, love? What is more than love?

Favor is Fair

If everyone gets grace and mercy, why do You even waste my time? Why are You always bugging me? I want to lash out. I want to beat people up. I want to let everyone know I am smart, and they are way too unintelligent to ever think they got over on me. Why can't I just do whatever? Why can't I just go shoot a couple of people, so they can understand they were dealing with a tamed beast this entire time? Why don't You let me off this leash?

BOY, YOU AND I BOTH KNOW THE WORLD DOESN'T NEED YOU NOT CARING ABOUT WHAT YOU DO. WE BOTH KNOW HOW EXTREME YOUR MIND IS AND CAN BE.

Ugh, God, You can be so annoying at times, I hope You know.

AS IF YOU AREN'T! REMEMBER, IT IS YOU ALWAYS GETTING IN MY WAY, NOT THE OTHER WAY AROUND.

I am saying though, I have done nothing but try to love these dudes, and look how they did me.

OKAY, RYAN, I WILL LET YOU HAVE YOUR MOMENT. WE HAVE ALREADY DISCUSSED SAMUEL.

I know, I know, they sinned against You and not him and he was just a messenger for You. So, he prayed for them once he realized it was You they offended. It was not himself, Samuel.

OKAY, THEN. YOU WANT TO BE IN YOUR FEELINGS.

It really sucks not being able to show rage, I hope You know.

I AM THE ONLY ONE WHO KNOWS HOW TO DEAL WITH IT, AND IT ISN'T HOW MOST OF YOU ALL THINK IT IS, EITHER.

I know, I know. You absorb hate and anger with love. The very thing You are doing right now. I get it.

WELL, WHY DON'T YOU UNDERSTAND THE FAVOR I HAVE PLACED UPON YOU?

The favor? Favor! Got it.

Life had sped up so fast, I forgot all about favor. How did I forget about favor? Favor is what I've sought the most. Favor is how I knew I was doing my Father's will. I can't believe life had stolen from me the foundation of everything I worked towards and strived for…favor. I quickly realized that grace and mercy were nothing in comparison to favor. I realized that the grace and mercy given to others robbed me of seeing the favor I had attained. I had faith, but I lacked the understanding.

I TOLD YOU, WITH ALL THY GETTING, GET AN UNDERSTANDING . YOU ALWAYS WANT TO RUN. I JUST WANT YOU TO WALK.

Well, I guess I have to give them the grace and mercy they deserve… or not.

RYAN!

You know I am joking, so I can return to favor.

There definitely isn't anything greater than love. However, we must learn how to recognize love. That four-letter word is the most overused, manipulated, misunderstood, powerful and meaningless word that is known to man. With so much emphasis given to it, by so many, for different intents and purposes, love is still what the entire world wants and searches for. We want it so badly that we change the definition and meaning of it, just so we can feel as though it is present in our lives. The word is under attack and has been under attack since its inception.

The very first time a word was invented to encompass how to act as Our Father wishes us to. The devil had to come up with a way to combat it. We all have our own version of the meaning of love. That is the biggest problem. Everyone wants to feel entitled to their opinion and version. We all need to realize and accept, everyone having their own opinion and version is the source of all foolishness. Maybe fewer people would have opinions, and more people would be able to get back to the truth if having an opinion was deemed being attached to the devil. Nonetheless, love must be our common ground. We must allow Our Father to define what love is, not ourselves.

We must allow Our Father to define what love is, not ourselves.

When we start to define love, we have to look at the biblical example of when Moses crossed the Red Sea. Any one of us who has ever run away out of fear, like running from a bumble bee or dog, as a child, knows there's that split second when we knew we could make it to our bike, or to look for a car's trunk or hood, for an escape. As long as we had a path in front of us, we were grateful. The Hebrews could have easily been grateful for low muddy waters when they crossed the Red Sea. Our Father gave them dry land instead.

Our Father has never short-changed anyone. He always creates a situation better than we could imagine, and that is favor. The truth is favor is how we can tell we are operating inside of His will. Favor is the response to our alignment with God. When we start to examine the truth behind this statement, the outlook can be gloomy or bright, depending on our perception.

The way to experience life is from our Spirit. Our Spirit is automatically associated with our thinking that controls our actions. We start to understand the power in decision-making. We take control of our lives by taking control of our thinking. We see that doing a little more than what is demanded of us, means we are constantly setting ourselves up for promotion. We also see how applying a little patience today allows for a lot of growth tomorrow.

We start growing and evolving in our lives. We are empowered via understanding why we need to control our thinking; it removes us from living in a state of defeat, and thinking as though we can't control our thoughts and thinking and therefore our lives. We start to learn from the results of life, as opposed to trying to dictate to life what the results should be. The frustrations we feel and get from life are due to a misalignment with Our Father's Spirit. Favor is a fact check of being inside the Holy Spirit.

We are to never confuse God's favor with man's. Joy, love, peace, longsuffering, gentleness, goodness, and meekness always allow you to enter into another's life on good terms and remain on good terms. We all want to identify ourselves as loving; in truth, few are willing to accept that entering and exiting a person's life is something that is not loving. We so earnestly seek to be perceived and understood as good and/or Godly. We overlook our flaws as opposed to dealing with them. Favor requires effort. Grace and mercy require us to show up. So many want the same results as those who put forth the effort, without putting forth the same effort. No matter the effort put forth by another, if any one individual doesn't put forth the same effort, no matter how much gain is exposed to them, they will never receive gain from it.

Even if we don't experience a certain truth, we must be willing to accept another's testimony of it. If we don't accept another's testimony of the truth, we will find ourselves living out the same truth. The result is experiencing the heartaches of life, due to judging another's failures, as opposed to learning from them. The very truth we all must accept is, we fail every time we lean on our own understanding. We never see our own wrongs, until we escape our own thinking . Our own thinking is what keeps us operating in the state of needing grace and mercy (sinning).

The very truth we all must accept is, we fail every time we lean on our own understanding.

As children, we could easily know and tell those around us loved us. We ran up to everyone, giving them hugs and smiles. The younger the child, the more innocent we assume them to be, so we naturally show more love to little kids. It is because we feel our love can be given and received freely. We all have the same innocence inside us, but over time, we become jaded from hurt and pain. We only feel comfortable expressing our true innocence with those we feel won't hurt us. An example is women who have had kids, catching baby fever when they're around the innocence of a baby too long. They remember releasing all of their worries and pains in the pure love they had with and for their children.

Due to the judgments and perceptions of the world, everyone feels the need to walk around with a filter, when everyone in the world wishes they could live free of a filter. No one really wants the world to know them by their past sins and errors, therefore the memory of our past sins become a mental prison the devil puts us in. Our past actions make us put ourselves in a box. The box that defines us limits what we can be. The limits automatically put fear into the mix. To extend beyond a boundary or border that we feel exists and is present, is always viewed as a hard task. We all must be willing to defeat our thinking and give it over to God's control. We all must view any boundary or border we have allowed to be present in our minds as a limit we have placed on God, Our Father.

To truly repent, we must return to our true innocence. We can't remember being completely innocent. The closest thing we can remember is back when we were younger. The only reason we can say that is because we can't really remember how we were. We just see a lot of kids, and all the kids we see are more loving, so we assume that's how we were too. We want to believe we were once pure and innocent. What we are really trying to do is regain an attachment to purity and innocence, by reflecting on a time we can't accurately remember in detail. We want to believe so strongly that we can be good. We continue to search for it inside of us, when we know everything we can remember is tainted.

The truth of the matter is, we have always been disobedient. Our disobedience is what separates us from God, Our Father. We must see past the identifying process of calling it sin. Recognize and see it to be what it truly is, disobedience. Sin and being disobedient go hand in hand. A person operating in sin must admit, it is because they are being disobedient. It seems like a simple concept, but until you view operating in sin as needing grace and mercy, you will never repent and gain favor. Likewise, operating in obedience gives us access to love in the form of favor. We can never truly identify how important it is for us to give ourselves over to Our Father at every moment.

We want to believe that trying is good enough. We want to believe that caring enough to even try should result in favor. We want to believe that any true effort we put forth should be rewarded on a grand scale or by some grand gesture. We are so full of sin and ourselves. We often view the smallest right being done as a tremendous amount of right being done. If we can pinpoint the times in life we did right, it is the same as a racist who has three friends of the opposite color and believes he or she is not a racist. So much focus and attention are given to the few to justify not having many. We give so much attention to when we were right, that we fail to see all the times we robbed ourselves of getting and receiving Our Father's favor. The entire premise boils down to this: Whose reward are we seeking?

If we were truly seeking Our Father's rewards, we would recognize that favor here on earth is one of them. So much attention and emphasis are put on making it into heaven; we forget about favor here on earth. We think we have to struggle throughout life on earth, in order to receive something better in heaven. In the *Lord's Prayer*, Jesus taught us to say, "Thy will be done on earth, as it is in heaven."

Once we understand the two must match, we start to pursue what it takes for them to match: What am I missing that prevents favor in my life? Is my disobedience detrimental to my growth ? Am I really getting in God's way that much? Can life really be as easy as God says it is and should be? God already understands I am a sinner, so why is He asking for the impossible? All these things can run through our minds when we think of the requirements of favor. Each time we receive favor, every time it is given to us, we leap with joy. We fail to realize God wants us all to become favorable in His eyes. Therefore, instead of us seeking favor as individuals, we finally understand to receive ultimate favor, we receive it as a group. He is communicating with us all via the Holy Spirit. If we are all vessels and hosts for Our Father's use, isn't it our ultimate purpose to show unconditional love to our fellow man?

Until we are willing to perform this ultimate act, we can't look for ultimate favor. In times when love is required of us, the "why me's?" and "do we really have to's?" can enter into our thinking. The answer is easy when our response is simply, "It is the loving thing to do." The "woe is me" concept is thrown out the window, when we admit and accept, we are more than overcomers. We are more than conquerors. The paths of life are many. The best outcome from life is one pathway, *the* pathway. The best life is a life lived in the Spirit of Christ, Our Father's Spirit, the Holy Spirit, the Holy Ghost.

The best life is a life lived in the Spirit of Christ, Our Father's Spirit, the Holy Spirit, the Holy Ghost.

Once we operate in this mindset, the thought of favor becomes a reality. How to achieve and maintain favor is a constant question that has a simple answer. At all times, we must perform the ultimate act of love, and so we are all to become charitable.

Receive Favor

I had to get back to the basics. Living life back in America sped up my life to the point, I stopped thinking. I had to abandon the fast pace most people lived by. I had to remember living fast without a connection would never get me anywhere. I would just run in place or in circles. I realized that a constant connection is what I needed.

REMAIN IN CONSTANT CONNECTION.

Remain in constant connection?

I remember this feeling all too well. Every step I made at one point felt connected to God, but now life seems to be a blur. I feel so disconnected by thinking I was connected the entire time.

YOU BECAME DISCONNECTED WHEN YOU CHOSE TO START THINKING APART FROM ME AGAIN.

Instead of listening to what I knew to do all along, I allowed others to corrupt my own thinking. As I sat in a hotel room, I was amazed at how things ended up with me, here and now. I was also amazed at the fact that I wasn't upset about it. I didn't know if it was because of the frequent hotel stays due to my job, or because of my acceptance of being defeated.

REMEMBER WHEN YOU WONDERED HOW PEOPLE COULD END UP LIVING IN A HOTEL...AND YOU JUDGED THEM FOR IT?

Wow! I forgot all about that.

STOP JUDGING.

Anything that I have ever said in ignorance, arrogance and out of stupidity, please, please, please, I beg of You, remove it from my path.

I accepted in an instant not to worry about how a person got where they were in life. In order to perform Our Father's will, I had to respect and love them anyway and regardless. I realized; we all can end up anywhere in life. It is only Our Father who saves us from hardships. I accepted I had to forgive again. I had to let go of any hidden anger or animosity. I accepted I had to be pure.

This time however, I realized true favor required more than just faith. It required acting with the understanding of the action. There is a huge difference between blindly doing something out of faith, and understanding, it is because of my faith I will perform this action.

Wow, if it wasn't for all this, I would have never received understanding.

YOU ASKED, I GAVE.

I know I really need to be careful what I ask for in the future. I can tell You that much. I understand I cannot add to You. I understand now I can only take away from Your presence and energy. I understand now, on my own accord, I cannot perform Your will. I became so lost in Your favor, I forgot it was Your favor and not mine. Sorry for getting in Your way.

YOU WILL AGAIN. YOU ALREADY KNOW YOU ARE FORGIVEN BEFORE IT EVEN HAPPENS. JUST COME BACK TO ME.

Come back to me?

At the moment I realized, in trying to become the best Ryan I could be, I became the worst version of the Holy Spirit. I became non-present in Spirit. Ryan was, and forever will be, tainted with the lust of the eye...the things that pull at my pride, ego, and vanity. Ryan's thinking is, and will forever be flawed, and less than Our Father's. I had to learn, as I blindly accepted before. Ryan and Our Father cannot exist at the same time. It is either going to be me or Our Father leading the decision-making process… thinking. I realized, I forgot to renew my mind . I forgot to say, "I am stupid; You are smart. I am foolish; You are wise. I am the sinner; You are my salvation."

WELL, RYAN, WITH THAT BEING SAID, WHAT'S UP WITH THESE RECORDS OF WRONGS OF OTHERS YOU HAVE OVER HERE? DO YOU REALLY WANT TO REPEAT THIS LESSON?

Thank you, Yahushua Ha Mashiach (Jesus)! Ha ha ha ha ha. You already know I don't want to go there. You can have it. I know, Father, you keep no records of wrong. I am getting rid of them for you right now.

WHAT ABOUT THIS LACK OF ZEAL AND ZEST FOR LIFE? YOU ARE MORE THAN AN OVERCOMER. YOU ARE MORE THAN A CONQUEROR. A LESSON IS A LESSON; YOU ARE TO LEARN FROM THEM, NOT LOSE YOUR HEART.

More than a conqueror? Don't lose my heart?

I realized, to receive favor, I couldn't have a "woe is me" mindset. I had to resume being a conqueror. Once again, I had seen and understood the trap of emotions. Each tug and pull on my emotions clouded my thinking and judgment . The more tugs and pulls, the cloudier the thinking. It was easy to lose my heart with the constant bombardment of what life should be and should consist of. All the advertising and marketing made me focus on what I didn't have, as opposed to the things I already possessed. It robbed me of doing the simple chasing after the extravagant. I thought and pondered for a little while longer, until I realized, I needed no more thinking and pondering. I just had to do the things I knew I was required to do. Favor is simply a byproduct of performing love. Favor leads to prosperity; it is not prosperity in itself.

YOU COULD BE IN JAIL RIGHT NOW OR ON THE STREETS. CAN I GET A "THANK YOU?"

Thank you.

DO YOU REMEMBER WHAT I SAID TO YOU AFTER YOU SAID YOU WERE GOING TO COST ME A QUARTER-MILLION DOLLARS?

If I lose that much in the name of love, just imagine what you will get in return.

STOP DOUBTING AND WATCH ME WORK.

A person operating in favor is quick to admit they are foolish. A person operating in favor will never try to take credit for what they are doing. They give all glory and honor only to Our Father, because they fully accept the favor really is His. When we start to accept who we are, versus who we want to be, we start to see some common truths and patterns throughout our lives.

No matter what vice a person has, it shows its face throughout their life. During childhood, if a little boy or girl isn't corrected and given the proper reasoning to not have a wandering eye, in the future, he or she will never be able to turn a blind eye to distractions. We can't expect someone who hasn't been taught to somehow magically act and operate correctly. When a certain behavior goes unchecked, we naturally build up our own reasoning for why it isn't as bad as others make it out to be. Because of this, all these traits and behaviors that go unchecked by loved ones, become strongholds in our adult lives.

To receive favor, we must identify a stronghold and be willing to repent (stop doing it). Our strongholds are different, yet the same. We all dibble and dabble in the same temptations, daily. We choose to become tempted by one thing or the other, minimizing our vices and highlighting the vices of others. The more vices we have; the more we highlight others' vices. We must do this to balance out the negativity in ourselves. We justify our negativity and evilness by saying that others have more. With all the negativity in the news and media, and all the drama on television and in movies, we can easily identify the seeds of negativity being planted in our lives. The more we think others have drama and negativity in their lives, the more we are willing to accept it in ours. The more we see it, the more we believe it to be real.

Marketing has established repetitiveness as an effective way to get someone's attention. Anyone with money can influence many others by repeatedly telling their story. It is then projected as truth. Put it into TV shows, the media, news, books and blockbuster movies, and every carnal-minded person in the world is quickly and easily convinced. Most may want to say that it isn't that simple. Sadly, all the wise ones out there admit that it is. The tearing down of anything begins mentally, with the hope that dismantling will affect us spiritually.

The breaking of someone's spirit is always mentioned and spoken of. Few take the time to really break down what that means. The breaking of someone's spirit should never be done. The breaking of someone's spirit means to force them to accept wrong as right, and right as wrong. We can see, with the use of propaganda, why it is so easy to influence others into sinful thinking. Once the world and society have said that something is normal and accepted, many feel forced to accept and treat it as normal, even when it goes against the core of Jesus' beliefs.

The truth is, we are always to be built up in the Holy Spirit, not torn down. To receive favor, we must be willing to do something other than what is projected as normal. We all know the level of what society projects as "normal" really varies, by citizen and by social class. Therefore, the extreme of normal is day-to-day working for minimum wage, which is something we all want to be above. We all have minds full of ideas and possibilities, so we all want to experience our own pursuit of happiness. These are our unalienable rights. Sound familiar?

The right to pursue our own happiness is something from God, Our Father. No one can ever claim responsibility for that. We all want to be great, but few of us truly imagine an outcome, situation, or world in which we are all great. Too many have imagined. They have achieved or possess such a greatness. They feel comfortable being great by themselves and above others. To receive favor, we must first define what it is to live in a world full of "prosperity." The new word for having a lot of mammon. Which means anything we have set aside for our own purpose. When we think of prized possessions, there are some things few are willing to share. Prosperity is a lie. It is nothing more than a trick of the devil. A lot of people fall victim to chasing after money, saying they want to be blessed.

Blessed are the poor and the meek. The Beatitudes explain a blessed individual, but they have nothing to do with prosperity in the material sense. Only someone willing to sell their soul to the devil can succeed in the devil's system (We will get into that later , but we might as well plant the seed now.). The devil is any human operating outside the Holy Spirit. Their thinking is linked to the flesh, therefore it is carnal and of the devil. Prosperity is just a marketing and advertising concept for convincing people that mammon can be good. Those who are not of the Holy Spirit but claim to be, make claims that the more mammon we have, the more God is with us. The Bible says that the more we worship mammon, the less we will be able to worship God. We must understand. If we have to search for the truth, we are obviously being fed and given a lie.

Only someone willing to sell their soul to the devil can succeed in the devil's system.

Favor isn't prosperity…Favor is favor…Favor can and will lead to prosperity, but prosperity in the form of resources for His Kingdom, not money and materialistic things for personal use. In a world full of discord, to be able to feel a slice of heaven on our own and in our own right, is to feel comfortable abandoning our brothers and sisters while they are being tormented. We all like to try to make it seem like it is another's fault for their hang ups. We want to claim to be our brother's and sister's keepers, but we are quick to come up with a reason not to help them, based on the past. We claim to want to be extra supportive, but out of the same mouth we say that we don't want to be foolish and give to sinners. Meanwhile, sinners are the ones who need to have love shown and displayed to them the most. The Holy Spirit inside of them needs to be fed. Therefore, we must show love to sinners.

The Bible says to not "cast your pearls before swine." Many want to make this out as a reason to not help others. However, pigs are those that will just devour the best of what you have. Many of us are so trusting, and this is the very thing we are doing right now without knowing it. Instead of planting seeds into a sinner's life and helping our brothers and sisters, we would rather give to some organization or charity that just runs through our money. We look back on how much was donated and wonder what was done with the funds. The best we had to give was something the group ran through and trampled upon.

We have to stop judging one another. We have to stop wanting to feel up by looking down. We must accept all the demons of life are on the inside, not the outside. The way we respond is what truly matters. The devil can tempt us however he may. It is up to us how we respond, once we understand that the devil is simply anyone who comes into our lives in an un-Fatherly fashion. It is easy to see how even we can, and have been, the devil in others' lives. We have all been Peter when Jesus told him, "Get thee behind me, Satan." We have all given someone some carnal advice, instead of saying what Our Father would have them do. We say, "I know what you mean. I feel you, and you know what? I can understand why you are sinning." When we think, we start blurring the lines. We automatically give ourselves over to a reprobate or a depraved mind.

A reprobate or depraved mind is simply us knowing right from wrong but choosing to accept wrong as right. We must accept when we lean on our own understanding, it automatically makes us a fool. Once we accept that our own thinking is our biggest problem, we let go of our past and our own thinking. When we become tired of operating in grace and mercy, we truly attain the right spirit to become humble enough to evolve. Right is right. There is no super right. The second we treat others as we would want them to treat us, we must accept that we all want to be treated as Our Father in Heaven treats us.

Once we finally accept, we are to do everything as pleasing in the sight of the Lord, not only can we tap into favor, but we can also understand it. Favor is reserved for someone operating inside the Holy Spirit. No one can reject the promotion of the person who is constantly going above and beyond. We may think they are gimmicky, or even stupid at times. Some of us think and view them as being ignorant. We think to ourselves, "If they only knew what they could be getting away with?" However, at the time of the promotion, we want to discredit all their extra effort because no one told them to do that. A non-spiritual mindset will never be able to digest this. The Holy Spirit always chooses to do its best, so it becomes us attaining the favor from others, due to the Holy Spirit interacting with them.

When we apply this concept on the job, we can easily see how, why, and where it works. We automatically see, by giving them more, they can't help but see we can do more. Our pride lies in knowing that we can do more and telling others how much better we would be at another's position, if given the chance or opportunity. Our humility resides in showing others how much more we can do, without broadcasting it or showing off. Once the humble man shows honor to Our Father, man will reward that individual for doing so.

When we go to work with a smile and perform to the best of our ability, day in and day out, being deserving of a promotion is a given in our minds. The smile and doing your best should be linked to God, not the possibility of a promotion. The problem lies with us getting into our feelings, when we are passed over. Instead of getting mad at ourselves for not trying our best and learning from the situation. We have the audacity to get mad at others, when we aren't being looked upon in the light, we think we deserve. We must accept the understanding of why it was foolish to try and get over. We have to stop looking to God, for things we didn't put forth effort to receive.

In friendships, we would edify one another. We would look out for people the way we want them to look out for us. We become considerate and understanding. Patience to get through any event with our friends is a given. Help and support would be the norm. Encouragement would just be a look, as opposed to a discussion. Loving smiles would replace faces full of discord. Friends would know we will tell them the truth. Bonds would be deeper, and we would appreciate others for their honesty. Friendships based in truth and love is what everyone wants, but we feel the need to lie in order to be cordial.

A friendship based in the Spirit has to be based in truth . Therefore, telling all our friends what they are doing wrong, in judgment, makes us have fewer friends. Likewise, telling all our friends their wrongs in love, will make others view us as their personal fixers and reliable sources of truth and wisdom. The more we deal with others in truth and love, the more favor they will have for us when they understand the fullness of the truth. The more we lie to them, the more they will say that we didn't have their best interest in mind. The wiser choice is to deal with others in truth and love.

In relationships and marriage, going the extra mile at all times unlocks deeper layers and levels of intimacy. When someone knows we are willing to go the extra mile for them, they in turn become willing to go the extra mile for us. We become connected on a spiritual level, once we reach unity in love. Hence the reason no man or woman can separate a Godly union. Instead, we have taken God out of marriage and wonder why we see so many divorces. We have stopped highlighting that the focus of marriage is to raise Godly children. For a child to receive proper rearing, he or she has to get the same response from both parents at all times, for one single truth to be established. When someone knows we are willing to go the extra mile for them, they in turn become willing to go the extra mile for us.

Any area of our lives where we aren't being spiritual will be pointed out by our mate. Therefore, we have to admit that the only one believing in our lies is ourselves. Our mates can automatically tell something is different by observing our body language and change of behavior. We hold on to so much guilt for things our mates have already forgiven us for. Since we haven't confessed to certain sins, the thought of our partner finding out is a constant worry. We can't admit the truth about ourselves to ourselves. Let alone, let it come out from our own lips to our partner. Therefore, we can never operate as if that lie doesn't exist. The more lies exist. The more separate the two become. The more we show love to our partner, the safer he or she will feel in being able to be truthful.

The security of knowing that someone has our back with unconditional love, is when we are willing to do anything for another. If we are secure in our relationship with Our Father, we must be willing to take on the true Spirit. Not only that, but we must then worship in Spirit and truth. We must all become Spiritually minded. The biggest lesson of life is realizing the Spirit that connects it all together. We all want to dissect life down to a microscopic level of understanding; We think the more in depth we go, the more we know. We fail to see the more microscopic we go, the smaller the overall picture becomes. It is better for us to understand the full story, before we start to shrink it down to moments in time.

Becoming Fatherly Minded

As the days turned to weeks, now months, I started to wonder if my path and my destiny were in alignment. I thought I was loving. I thought I was doing a good thing. I chose love when others were telling me I was crazy and stupid for doing so. I realized the trap in me was not thinking my destiny was getting fulfilled. It was my tainted version of what man had given me, not the examples set forth by Our Father. The world we live in today says we should be prosperous if we are spiritually-minded . The question of how I could be spiritual and broke kept entering my mind. At one point in my life, money had become an afterthought. How is it now that I have none?

WHAT ABOUT JOSEPH?

For a week straight, Joseph was on my mind. I reread his story and came to the following conclusions: Joseph always had favor, even when his circumstances, from the outside looking in, didn't appear as such. I started thinking about all the people I had met, and I realized that each individual placed in my life increased my zest, zeal, and passion for performing my Father's will. I realized the need for the mission my faith took on but without understanding. I chose to ask for understanding. I began to understand that having a spiritual mind is the true blessing and favor.

I was led to the Apostle James. Trials and tribulations come to make you stronger. That is when everything hit me.

What happens if you are already strong?

Favor is never the reason for pursuing anything. The real reason to pursue any task is whether it will help our fellow man. When the reason we pursue our goals is defined, the energy it takes to fulfill that task has to match. The only way for me to tap into the energy for Our Father's will to be done, was to awaken everyone else to their own energy. This seemed far-fetched and unreasonable at first. The more and more I dug into what the Spirit was revealing to me, the more it made sense.

I had to wash all my thinking and thoughts against what I knew Our Father would want me to do. I realized that my Father does not care about worldly possessions, but about the transgressions we are committing towards Him and each other. He wants us to spread love. Therefore, if we succumb to measuring life by man's judgments and measurements, we are already using the wrong scale. Our Father wants us to be held accountable to love. Our Father measures a successful day by whether we were charitable, positive, and helpful to our fellow man.

I realized the trap I had fallen in. I forgot whose reward and approval I was seeking. I started to understand the purpose of me living in different settings. I had chosen to come back from overseas and live isolated and by myself, having no contact with anyone but my wife and sons. I had prayed so earnestly in the desert to attain a message to save the people, but I abandoned the people in my actions. I cut access to the message Our Father had given me from those who needed it most. The events in life made me begin to understand all the things I so zestfully signed up for. It was to solidify in me whether I wanted to live for Our Father or throw in the towel and live for myself.

I had already experienced some mild comfort in life. It would be easy for me to return to it.

I TOLD MY DISCIPLES TO TAKE NOTHING WITH THEM. THE PROVISIONS FOR THEIR JOURNEY WILL BE GIVEN TO THEM.

At that moment I knew I couldn't equate money in my bank account to favor from Our Father. The first step in becoming spiritually minded is to admit our transgressions. We would like to think this is easy. However, we tend to turn a blind eye to obvious wrongs when it comes to our own transgressions. We tend to look at all the things society stresses towards us: I have a job; I have a career; I have a house or an apartment; I have a car; I try my best to take care of my responsibilities; I am law-abiding; and last but not least, the only people who have an issue with me are people who don't have their stuff together. We rack and stack ourselves with comparisons towards others to see if we measure up spiritually. Everything we do begins with us projecting outward to have some form of understanding of how we feel about ourselves, but none of this makes us look in the mirror.

To become spiritually minded, we must be on an honest quest to start perfecting ourselves. This is called bearing our own cross. Once we bear our own cross, we are willing to admit all our flaws, not just a few. We must admit, we already know right from wrong. We have to admit it is just us choosing not to do what we know to be right. We must admit, due to our own thinking, we have seen it invaluable and unreasonable to fully do what is right and commanded to us. We all understand how valuable we are. We all feel as though not being allowed to operate at our full potential is unfulfilling. Therefore, if someone robs one of us of our full potential, they rob us of our full reward.

Our pride and carnality have a way of appearing as reasoning in the way we think. Until we understand that it is our own reasoning that makes us carnal, we can neither understand nor admit that we bring the devil to the table. We all do. We are the ones who bring doubt, fear, resentment, laziness, procrastination, unforgiveness, envy, hate, coveting, lusting, and a laundry list of other negative and unhelpful emotions, thoughts, and actions to the table. We are the ones who are outside of Our Father's will, therefore outside of His thinking. Once we admit that we are outside, we can start the process of working towards getting back inside. A spiritual mind must then admit, a Fatherly mind is the only mindset to have. "What would Jesus do?" is the same thing as, "What would my Father in heaven do?" Once we understand that Our Father will neither leave nor forsake us, we can accept that through the Holy Spirit is how He fulfills this promise.

Until we admit we should operate in perfection, we will never attain operating in Our Father's Spirit. We have destined ourselves to be lukewarm.

A lukewarm individual wants to allow their right to be accounted for tremendously, but their wrong to be swept under the rug and never discussed again. We do this all the time with family, friends, co-workers, and associates. We want them to get over our mistakes and concentrate on our good. The moment someone calls us out on our wrong, we become scorners, as if we were beyond reproach. Then, when someone points out our wrongs , we will do our best to point out theirs and call them haters. The issue with a lukewarm mind is, it is still attached to carnality. A lukewarm mind's understanding of right and wrong is very flawed; it appears or develops when we have come up with our own belief system. It is reprobate and depraved. We begin to operate with a little truth and a lot of lies.

We must separate ourselves from being lukewarm by becoming a willful baby in Spirit. We have to admit we don't know. We must admit that every time we tried to add a little something, or tweak the formula a little bit, it blew up in our faces. Once we admit that our lukewarm nature has been the reason for all our downfalls, we are finally ready to evolve past being lukewarm. We accept that we are foolish when we lean on our own understanding. We accept that we must hate the fact we can't get right. We accept that we can't do it on our own. We conclude that we need to lean on something greater than ourselves. We see how full of sin we truly are. We realize that we ourselves are sinful . The only thing that can save us is the Holy Spirit.

We are all the biggest liars, cheaters, schemers, and get over artists out there in our own right. Whatever we are choosing to get over on, we do it so effortlessly that we don't even realize we are doing it. We are the ones who don't want to follow. Once we admit it is only due to our willingness to be obedient in some areas, do we excel at them. Will we receive the vision to see, it is our disobedience that causes us to fail.

We must accept right and wrong is something outside our control. It is something we must accept as law. Grasping right and wrong as something everyone easily sees and understands is hard for a person constantly trying to get over. They continue to think they are smarter than others, and people believe their lies. Therefore, robbing others of the truth of their lying prevents them from receiving proper correction.

Disobedience is sin to our fellow man. Every time we sin, we don't have our fellow man at heart. Every time we do something wrong, someone else is affected in a negative way. A spiritually minded individual will never want to be a stumbling block to their neighbor or do things to cause another to go astray. We must recognize that separation and division are of the flesh. All our thinking of separation and division must depart. The Body of Christ separates itself spiritually, not physically. The spiritual mind must be embedded in society to be a beacon of light in a world full of darkness. The spiritual mind is Our Father's will, and it must be there for the just and unjust alike. The Holy Spirit has already been released. We must start fully believing in it.

To know, without a doubt, if we have a Fatherly mindset, the easiest thing to do is ask ourselves if we are being completely loving. Oftentimes, we have to admit we aren't. We must be able to recognize when we fall short of Fatherly love. Unconditional, selfless love is required of those living inside of, and from the Holy Spirit. You can't claim to be in and of Our Father's Spirit, and not possess His love.

The truth of, "Am I loving?" cuts deep. Love is clearly defined. Shall I say charity? Love is something everyone believes in. Charity is love on spiritual steroids. Charity is giving out love for free, with no expectations in the physical form. We must arrive at charity to mature in the Spirit. Even sinners love those who love them; to become Fatherly-minded, we must love those who despise and hate us.

Our Father wants us to have and keep everyone in mind. Our own thinking limits love to ourselves. However, when asked to have love and compassion for a stranger, suddenly the question of why can come to mind. The past can easily create enough negativity, so we do not embark on the best future. These thoughts are ungodly and of the devil. To take something spiritual and make it about flesh is wrong. To worship in the Spirit, the flesh is abandoned. If the flesh is abandoned and the Spirit is received, why would anyone's physical appearance matter? We would know the Holy Ghost allows for the thoughts of others to be in the forefront of our minds, just like Our Father. Once we have others in the forefront of our minds, the value in unity increases tremendously.

When we start living for Our Father and not for ourselves, everyone we know is constantly on our minds , whether we're aware of it or not. It becomes a part of our subconscious to look out for people. When someone has an issue and we know someone who offers the services to assist and help, we recommend them quickly. We aren't out looking for ways to further or enhance our own success. We start helping others in their pursuit of their happiness.

When we come to the complete understanding of the Holy Spirit, we understand how and why we can't be selfish. Selfishness is a result of putting ourselves above others. We fill our minds with questions and statements like: It isn't my fault. Why do I have to? What does it matter to me? Why should I care? If they wanted help, they would get it. All of these thoughts revolve around us as an individual. As long as our thoughts revolve around ourselves, our thoughts will never be able to revolve around anything else. The Holy Spirit is something that must be accepted. It will be easy in some areas and rather difficult in others. The devil likes to point out our good to justify our flaws. The devil will have us believing we are doing Our Father's will, yet all the while, we know we are cheating and getting over.

A look in the mirror in all areas of life is what's demanded of everyone wanting to live in a Fatherly way. To become spiritual, and to live out of and from the Holy Spirit, are two totally different things. To become spiritual is just starting the process of having the ability to start thinking. Our spirit, the Holy Spirit, and our salvation are very dependent on each other. If our thinking is not right, our spirit will be in turmoil. If our spirit isn't right, we will never possess the ability to give ourselves over to the Holy Spirit. Then our souls will never be at peace, because we fail to think, act, and respond as the Holy Spirit directs us.

To become spiritual, and to live out of and from the Holy Spirit, are two totally different things.

Once we separate ourselves from right and wrong, we have a clear understanding of what is right and wrong. We now can choose to operate in what is right. When we operate in what we know to be right, it is now up to others to correct us in our pursuit of the Holy Spirit. We should gladly receive and take these corrections. However, when we are operating carnally, we will lash out and feel superior to the person trying to correct us.

The Spirit we should operate in, once we accept Jesus/Yeshua as our Lord and Savior, is the Spirit of the LORD of Hosts. Galatians Chapter 5 states the fruit in this way: If our lives are not full of love, joy, peace, long-suffering, gentleness, goodness, faith, meekness, and temperance, we must admit we aren't living in, but out of Our Father's Spirit.

If we aren't experiencing the fruit, we must examine our thinking and actions against Our Father's purpose and will. Once we start the process of self-checking and renewing our mind, refinement and perfection will naturally happen. The refinement and perfection processes are where the purpose of it all is revealed.

DAY
TWO
LEARNING HOW TO WALK

Spiritual Refinement

Money is not the goal for my life. I have a need for money, but the only need I have for money is the ability to acquire more resources.

YOUR BROTHERS AND SISTERS ALREADY HAVE THE RESOURCES.

I had to grow, so I could understand, the things I kept asking of my Father were already there. I quickly changed my thinking into what I had to do to come into contact with all the provisions He set up for me in my life. I then realized, He left me a road map to interact with my brothers and sisters. I realized the road map was me acting in love.

Once I understood anything outside of a loving attitude, personality and vibe, others would recognize me as sketchy, stuck up, or as though something wasn't quite right about me. I was able to see, plain as day, giving love is the key to receiving love from anyone. "It is better to give than to receive," became clear. I had to give out unconditional love in order to receive it.

UNLIMITED LOVE!

Ok, I had to learn to give unlimited love, so I could feel as though I was worthy of accepting unconditional love. Conditional, limited love is what the world offers; that is love based on conditions I meet or achieve. God showed me that the conditions I set on my love were how I became worldly. I realized, God's love is unlimited and without conditions. It is either given as grace and mercy, or as favor. I saw myself applying conditions on the love I gave as what truly weakened the power of love in my life. Once I applied to others the same view Our Father had towards me, I saw that we all act as Our Father without knowing it.

I TOLD YOU I HAD CONTROL OF THEIR HEARTS. WHY DID YOU DOUBT IT?

Throughout the years, I've seen how everyone withholds favor from a sinner. They just don't tell the person sinning against them, the reasons they treat them outside of favor. By society adopting the meaning of love on such a superficial level, society has lost sight of what God commands of us. We have confused Our Father loving us with us automatically gaining favor. The love Our Father has for us, in the form of grace and mercy, allows us to repent and change.

I often scoffed at such a "basic thing," but I had to admit I couldn't truly forgive and offer grace and mercy to others. That seems minimal when it comes in the form of a reward and receiving it. When it comes in the form of giving it out to others, however, it is impossible on my own accord. Grace and mercy are reserved for sinners. Every time someone sins against me, my reply should always be love in the form of grace and mercy. When someone has wronged me, the last thing I will think on my own accord is forgiveness. My thinking without God's intervention is rooted in anger, frustration, and aggravation. In those moments of frustration, aggravation, and anger, I knew to call on God, because I knew I couldn't handle or take it. He has never failed to send His peace and comfort, so I can perform the action of love.

I started to see that the entire purpose of me learning about charity and love, was to be able to effectively perform His will, which is the entire purpose of my life. I realized that my dreams and goals had to be replaced with His. I could no longer think of my life as my own. I realized, in accepting His ways over mine, I accepted His thoughts and actions over mine as well.

Thank you for all the frustrating people you sent along the way.

FRUSTRATING?

Yes! You know how aggravating it is to be following after You, and someone comes along and says I can be doing more or better?

YOU COULD HAVE, **AND** THEY WOULDN'T HAVE BEEN FRUSTRATING IF YOU WEREN'T BEING PRIDEFUL.

I thought about everything the Holy Spirit had placed on my heart and in my spirit. I realized that trying to build my own private escape was not God's will. I realized that God's will deals with His children. It is collective and inclusive; it deals with us all. I realized, in order for God's Kingdom to exist, it had to have a network.

Am I available to everyone that is in God's network?

REMEMBER ALL THOSE PEOPLE YOU HAVE PASSED ALONG THE WAY WITH IDEAS THAT ADDED TO YOURS?

You mean to tell me all those people? That is a lot of reconnecting. What about all the people I reached out to, but I was of no help?

ARE YOU REALLY ASKING ME THIS WHEN YOU ALREADY KNOW THE ANSWER?

So, You're telling me I have to go the extra mile no matter what?

WOULDN'T YOU WANT SOMEONE TO DO IT FOR YOU? YOU HAVE TO ACCEPT. THE SAME LOVE YOU WANT FROM ME IS THE LOVE I REQUIRE OF YOU.

That means I must love with no limits or conditions too.

I GIVE YOU THIS NEW COMMANDMENT, TO LOVE AS I HAVE LOVED YOU. IT HAS BEEN THERE ALL ALONG. YOUR JOB IS TO SHOW LOVE, NOT SEARCH FOR IT.

The refinement and perfection processes are aggravating and tedious. Until we become spiritually aware of what is taking place, nit-picking and pointing out minor flaws can be extremely frustrating. The problem with the perfection stage of life is it can make many of us backslide and repeat life lessons we've already learned. The purpose of living in the Holy Spirit is to teach us how to interact with each other. When we learn how to interact with each other, we can finally start the process of building up Our Father's Kingdom.

Once we start the process of becoming and operating in Our Father's Spirit, the Holy Spirit, we learn key pieces of information about life that relate to us all. We learn, at all times, no matter what state we are in, we want to be respected. Not only do we want to be respected, but we want to also be treated with respect. When we start to become completely honest with ourselves, we can start to identify the similarities between ourselves and others. When we start to see the commonality and not the differences, we automatically understand the 'why' and 'how' behind wanting to always be treated with love and respect.

We can identify certain periods of life when someone with a judgmental mindset could have treated us without respect; as a matter of fact, some did. We lost respect for them and gained respect for those who treated us with respect. Once we grasp that, we start to understand; we can't build Our Father's Kingdom without first respecting and loving others. Once we have the level of respect and love we ought to have by operating inside the Holy Spirit, we can finally get to the point where we truly love others in the Godly form.

We must first admit that it is impossible to show love to someone we don't respect. This is why the world would have us looking and focusing on others' wrongs. Once we admit and see faults in others, our carnal mind automatically loses respect. A carnal mind is also a judgmental mind. When we evaluate others, we automatically risk losing love and respect for them. If we don't respect someone, it is impossible for us to view them as a beneficial piece to the puzzle.

YOUR JUDGMENT MUST GO, IN ORDER FOR MY LOVE TO APPEAR.

Our judgment limits how beneficial someone can be to us. Judgment is only present, when our love is absent.

Everyone can be beneficial. It is up to us to build a person up so they can serve their intended purpose. Until we respect a person, we can never show the proper love it takes to get to know them. Giving love and respect is the only way to see value in any person we meet. No matter the current circumstances, we will be able to see worth inside any individual. We are always in a position to be able to encourage the good in others. We have to allow the encouragement of good to naturally take its course in getting rid of the bad. When we encourage good/right, a person automatically understands what is bad/wrong within themselves. Over time, as we show a person how valuable they are, they will automatically get rid of their own personal demons of feeling unworthy or incapable of doing good. They naturally start to overcome evil with good.

The more we tap into our brothers and sisters who are abandoned, the easier it is to develop numbers and a team. Our Father doesn't want us to forget about the poor. He does not want us to beg the rich. Once we understand, the poor have all the power. We can finally network on the level Our Father wants; we can then build His Kingdom. We are to see anyone in need as a soul needing an opportunity for life. We can start giving them life by presenting opportunities . Jesus promised us life, and life more abundantly. The man at the bottom is filled with the Holy Spirit.

To understand Our Father's Spirit, we must understand what goes against Our Father. Mammon is clearly against Our Father's wishes for us. We must understand mammon. Too many have fallen victim to thoughts of prosperity. The Bible clearly states, it is easier for a camel to enter through the eye of a needle than it is for a rich man to enter heaven. The issue with mammon is this: We want to possess worldly riches. Our Father says to store up heavenly riches. The second we take it upon ourselves to spoil ourselves, that becomes resources we take from Our Father's use.

Our Father's will trumps our own will of spoiling ourselves. When we stop chasing after worldly possessions, we can finally give over that time, energy, and effort to doing Our Father's will. Any individual chasing money will quickly step over what is right. Furthermore, to chase after money automatically changes our morals and values. It becomes imperative for us to acknowledge the true reasons behind our pursuit of life. The tides of man's money can change quickly.

- To invest simply to become rich is a trick of the devil.
- To save our entire lives and not do anything with the resources our spiritual Father has given us is immoral.
- To have tons of resources and not contribute to the greater good, is wrong.
- To try and capitalize upon our brothers' and sisters' ignorance, is sinful.
- To think Our Father is blessing us, specifically with the intentions of allowing us to live better than everyone else, is erroneous.
- To think we are covered in giving just because we helped our close family in times of need, is wrong.
- To think promoting someone is giving them a job so they can make the company more profitable, is incorrect.

Until we are ready to get rid of these errors, we will not be ready to get rid of sin, for to be in error is to be in sin. To make Our Father's Kingdom revolve around money is one of the biggest sins of all. When we look at sin as error, we can easily see how money prevents us from doing the Godly thing. Our Father commands us to give; our money will ask us if we are sure. Our Father says to help; our money will ask us why we should create competition. Our Father says to give our time in order to be helpful; money says we can make more money than another, therefore our time is more valuable than theirs. Pay somebody.

To make Our Father's Kingdom revolve around money is one of the biggest sins of all.

Money then starts to dictate to us who is "worth" our time. Money starts to dictate who looks the right part. Money starts to eliminate those with huge potentials for growth, and in turn makes us justify writing them off by simply saying, "You are just not ready yet." Money has already started to become the ruler of our lives. This is not done simply by looking for more money to have, but through the things we can buy with it. Our world starts to revolve around the next best thing or the next thrill.

Our happiness becomes reliant on what entertainment our money can afford. Our mood then becomes driven, based on the last time we were able to spend freely. We automatically chase the time in life when we were able to buy anything. The high times of life are centered on the last time we closed a big deal, or even worse, the last time we were able to impress others with our finances. Money creates an image of life that isn't real. It allows for one to feel superior to another. It automatically makes us compare our situation with others' situations.

God, Our Father, the Holy Spirit, wants us to build a Kingdom that surpasses a network built upon money. We must be ready for our Kingdom to revolve around Him. To have a Kingdom revolving around Him, we must first free ourselves from ourselves, and from our own thinking. If we build Our Father's Kingdom on our own accord, it will be free of what Our Father could and would build for us. We can't build a more complete Kingdom than the one He would provide for us. The network we already have is the foundation for Our Father's Kingdom. We just need Our Father's correction. Our network could be as immense as God's Kingdom, or it could be as small as we make it.

We can now see the tricks, traps, and devil's schemes behind keeping our circle small. Our circle was never supposed to be small. The only person who needs a small circle is a sinner. A sinner's ego and pride are dependent on their evaluation of themselves. No one in the carnal mind wants to hear something that goes against their ego. However, someone walking inside the Holy Spirit is ready to hear any minor tweaks and fixes that will make them excel in life and will include the patience to plant seeds in others' lives. When we limit our interactions with those around us, we never truly know who Our Father placed in our lives to slingshot us forward. When we lower our pride and ego, we can finally understand our purpose is to perform Our Father's will and build up His Kingdom.

It is only when our purpose and Our Father's will align, can we truly see supernatural growth. When determining our purpose, we can build with us in mind or with Our Father in mind. As long as we build with us in mind, our network will never be complete, nor as big as it is supposed to be or is intended to be. Even further, it will not include all the people who are meant to be in it. Lastly, our network will never be what it is supposed to be if we fail to allow Our Father's Spirit to lead it.

If unlimited, unconditional love isn't the glue holding any network together, the network isn't part of God's Kingdom. If a network full of unconditional, unlimited love, with Our Father's Spirit leading it comes along, it is easy to see why all networks without unlimited love will fail. Furthermore, we are not to be like the builders before us, who rejected the true cornerstone. Until we accept and understand, the true cornerstone is Our Father's Spirit. We will always be inferior to the kingdom we build within Our Father's will.

Our purpose should be to fulfill Our Father's will, not our own. If a network full of life, joy, love, peace, gentleness, goodness, and faith comes along, we can easily see how it would trump most networks of today to we can easily see how it would trump the networks, societies and economic systems of today. Just think about a network that includes long-suffering towards sinners. Our Father's Kingdom includes long-suffering. When we suffer the sins of a sinner, we can finally give them the love needed for them to repent. If a thief steals from an endless supply, the thief sees his or her foolishness and decides not to steal on their own. We must become the endless supply the sinner needs. Our Father's will has already left provisions for the sinner. We must learn to love the sinner and hate the sin.

Our Purpose

After much soul-searching, I came to the conclusion I already knew, I have no purpose on my own. Many people I spoke to around this transition time were confused by my smile and the words that came out of my mouth, and understandably so. With a smile on my face, I was discussing that I had no purpose. If I die today, I have insurance. My family would be ok. My job has several others who can perform my duties. There are plenty of loving individuals out there to pass love on to my sons. If I died, the thoughts I invoked in others would still live on. The only true purpose I could have was fulfilling my Father's will. Anything short of supplying the love and positive energy in me onto and into others would be meaningless.

I finally understood. The reason all my personal endeavors failed, was because they were personal. I was trying to build up my own mammon, while I was building up Our Father's Kingdom. I finally understood that the two did not match, not even close! The purpose of my life was never for me, but for the betterment of us. Until I connect with the rest of the Body of Christ, my life will forever feel meaningless. Once I took on Our Father's Spirit, my personal goals and passions had to conform to His will. I had to willfully take on the charge to pursue His will. Once I took this step, His will was revealed to me.

I know a lot of people think no man can understand the things of the Father, and I would totally agree with them. I would then say to everyone. Only carnality identifies with the flesh, which is how we all identify ourselves as men. Why, if we are striving to be spiritual, will we then be held back by the flesh? Once we step into the Holy Spirit, the rules obviously change.

John 15:

> **12)** This is my commandment, that ye love one another, as I have loved you. **13)** Greater love hath no man than this, that a man lay down his life for his friends. **14)** Ye are my friends, if ye do whatsoever I command you. **15)** Henceforth I call you not servants; for the servant knoweth not what his lord doeth: but I have called you friends; for all things that I have heard of my Father I have made known unto you. **16)** Ye have not chosen me, but I have chosen you, and ordained you, that ye should go and bring forth fruit, and that your fruit should remain: that whatsoever ye shall ask of the Father in my name, he may give it to you . **17)** These things I command you, that ye love one another.

I am not blind to my Father. He chose me to go through this life.

I DIDN'T TELL YOU TO CHOOSE THOSE PATHS, THOUGH.

I know you didn't. I am just happy I am here.

The paths I chose to take were my own stumbling blocks, and they were due to my not wanting to be completely obedient to the things the Holy Spirit was giving me. I understood life was something to learn from, by being observant and accepting of the truth. On the other hand, I could choose to experience negativity firsthand, just by thinking I was smarter or better than others who went down an erroneous road. The path to our purpose is already laid out in front of us. Once we accept Our Father's Spirit, our purpose is to perform His will over ours. His will is for us to give up our own free will and to serve Him.

The true battle I faced with this acknowledgement was truly dying to myself. I thought I had died to myself many times before. However, I realized I always kept a piece of myself around. I never was completely willing to die to myself. I wanted to keep the good things of Ryan. I wanted to still attach myself to what I saw in the mirror. What I have seen in the mirror can never be what my Father intended me to be. My Father, which is unseen, wants the Spirit inside of me, which is unseen, to come into acknowledgement of who and what He truly is…Our Father, the Creator of everything, and therefore the Creator of me. When I accepted that I was a spiritual being having a human experience, I was finally able to perform the will of my Father, by becoming His son.

His son?

ARE YOU NOT A CHILD OF GOD? ARE YOU NOT A PART OF THE BODY OF CHRIST? DOES NOT MY WORD SAY, FOR ALL WHO ARE LED BY MY SPIRIT ARE MY SONS?

What is our purpose? This question has confused and engulfed a lot of people's minds and spirits. We often beg and cry out to Our Father, in hopes of understanding what our purpose is and how we can fulfill His will. We search ourselves and the world around us to see where we fit in. We start to compare our strengths and weaknesses in an effort to find some sort of understanding. Most of us fall short by trying to learn of ourselves, as opposed to learning of Our Father's will. Many who strive to be Christian and/or spiritual have said *The Lord's Prayer*, but few understand in it, He gave us His will.

The Bible says, we must serve Him in spirit and truth. In addition, we learn it is with our minds, we serve the law of God. With the flesh, we serve the law of sin. We must first tackle our minds in order to properly deal with our flesh. We must ask ourselves if we have been willing to change our minds. In order to deliver this message, it is key that we understand the difference between becoming saved and operating in our salvation. Our Father's will is for us all to operate in our salvation. We must start the process of understanding our salvation, above being saved.

All of us are already saved because of the acts of our Savior Jesus Christ, Yeshua, Yahshua, Yahshua Ha Mashiach. Once we comprehend that we are already saved, we need to believe in His message for us to possess our salvation. We need to evaluate whether we are operating as though we are saved. A lot of people can honestly admit they aren't operating in their salvation. Many, however, fail to understand what it means, or what it takes to operate in our salvation. To operate in our salvation, we must admit that we are already saved. Once we admit that we are saved, we can finally bear our own cross.

To bear our own cross, we must accept all of our actions. Once we accept all of our actions, we can accept our sinful state. When we accept the truth that Our Father does not sin, we can finally identify our sins. Once we identify our sins, we can identify the areas of life where we are unFatherly. When we see the areas of life where we are unFatherly, it becomes our task to repent and change them.

When we see the areas of life where we are unFatherly, it becomes our task to repent and change them.

This is the perfection process. The salvation process is to operate completely from Our Father's Spirit. We now understand; it is inside us. However, it is up to us to accept Our Father's instructions and be obedient to them. When we are following and being obedient to Our Father's Spirit, the Holy Spirit, we possess our salvation.

Another way to look at this is to look from the perspective of saved versus rescued. We are all already saved. However, not all of us are rescued. When we become rescued, we have possession of our salvation. If we are all lost at sea, all our spirits would be on display. Everyone has become shipwrecked, but we all were given life jackets and rafts. There will be some who understand they can't swim. They won't ever take off their life jackets, let alone exit the raft. There will be some who say, "It's boring in the raft, I want to get in the water." They will exit the raft and use their life jackets as their source of protection. Some of them will take off their life jackets and want to swim on their own. When the waves of the ocean start to swell, all those who chose to abandon the raft will quickly and surely miss it.

There will be some who will claim to be expert swimmers. They will abandon the life jacket and raft, to impress others with their swimming capabilities. They will want to be praised for their efforts. There are those who will choose to be lukewarm in the water with the life jacket, so they will feel safe enough to abandon the raft. They will be the ones who are shocked the most. Even with the signs of the skies getting dark and the wind picking up, they will refuse to return to the raft, feeling they are in a safe enough swimming distance to get back. When the waves swell, and the highs and lows become great, they will quickly realize why they shouldn't have left the comforts of the raft.

Our Father's love is our ego's biggest problem. When Our Father sends out signs of His love to warn us, our egos take the opportunity to submit only to a safe distance; we will never fully be in the raft when we survive the warning waves. Warning waves are scary. We can do two things at this point in life: Understand why we should all be in the raft or be individuals choosing to boost their egos by surviving the waves.

Our egos will use the same waves of warning, as the reasons we can now swim further out. Our egos can become boosted to venture even further out. It is only when the highs and lows become too great do our egos become willing to submit and acknowledge its wrongs. The bigger our egos get, the bigger the waves must be to prevent us from going in the wrong direction. Experiencing extreme highs and lows without God makes us understand the need to be in the raft.

Even so, we all are still lost at sea. When everyone realizes we are saved but we aren't rescued, we can start the process of making it back to land. Being lost in the ocean is the same as being in the wilderness. The only way to escape the wilderness is to be rescued. We can stop trying to swim as individuals, and instead be rescued as a group. Those who are in the rafts can build things to signal for help. Those in life jackets can accompany someone diving, so the two could look for supplies together. Everyone could do what they comfortably feel like doing, but as a team, all are serving a purpose greater than themselves. Trying to survive by ourselves makes us useless to the whole.

The transition from being saved to operating in our salvation is similar. For instance, tying the rafts together, rescuing all those who grew tired of swimming and diving, swimming to find supplies for the group's use, working together to piece something together to signal for help, are steppingstones to becoming rescued. Both the vain and the just are performing the same acts. The intentions behind actions reveal true motives, not the actions themselves. One scenario results in still needing to be rescued, due to personal gain and pleasure. The other is working together to become rescued.

Once a boat comes along and rescues everyone lost at sea, going back to our selfish ways is simply to backslide into being a sinner again. It took teamwork and a calm manner to get through being lost at sea and rescued. It will be erroneous to think, once we are on land, we will require something different. Once we become rescued, we must keep the same approach that got us there. Once we take on Our Father's Spirit, we must keep it. To go back to our carnal version is to give up on our salvation. We become saved by believing in Jesus' teachings, and by keeping them near us. His words are constantly meant to be in our mouths and in our hearts.

To go back to our carnal version is to give up on our salvation.

Our faith is what saves us, the faith that He, Himself (Jesus), was risen from the dead. We possess our salvation when we receive the Spirit He died to release. Jesus already saved us all. To possess the Holy Spirit is to possess Our Father's thinking. We must accept our purpose, which is to not only to possess Our Father's thinking, but also to perform His will.

Our Father revealed His thinking by giving us *The Lord's Prayer* via Jesus, our Savior. "Our Father" goes deeper than most allow. Our Father is not God. Jesus never prayed to God, nor referred to God as God, unless He was trying to relate His Father to others. Jesus said those who are of God, hear God's words. This can be confusing to many. Until we accept God as Our Father, to hear a word from Our Father is common. To hear a word from God is rare. If Jesus said, "Our Father," we must realize God is Father to us all. To say, "Our Father" is to accept we are all one in the Spirit. Therefore, our purpose as Christians must be uniting, not tearing down and/or separating. We are all Our Father's children, whether we are obedient or not. The Holy Spirit is trying to guide us back to our Spiritual Father, the Creator, and governor of life.

Father to All

I met the first person, in person, who believed in the alien theory. I knew it existed, but I never tried to understand it. As I was driving to Aspen for work, I had a curious spirit.

Why, when an angel came down from heaven, was the man it came to visit always told, 'Fear not?' I thought an angel appearing is confirmation You exist. If I were visited by an angel, I would be excited as all get out. I would know everything was real. Fear not…I would be thinking I was the man and must be extra important. hahahahahaahhahaha

RYAN, SHUT UP! IF YOU SAW AN ALIEN, YOU WOULD DEFINITELY WRECK RIGHT NOW, AND PROBABLY POOH ON YOURSELF.

Hahahahahahahahahahahahahahaha, you got that.

It was then that my mind was opened to truly realizing they are one in the same. Both descended from the heavens. Both came giving man knowledge. It is kind of crazy, but I can dig it.

DID YOU ASK ?

Cool.

WHY ARE YOU CONSTANTLY CURIOUS ABOUT THINGS THAT SERVE NO PURPOSE FOR THE NOW? WHEN WILL YOU REALIZE I WANT YOU TO CREATE HEAVEN?

Instantly, a shocked look came on my face.

THINK ABOUT EVERYTHING YOU WANT TO ACCOMPLISH… FOOD IN ABUNDANCE, FREE FLOWING OF KNOWLEDGE, EVERYONE WORKING TOGETHER, PROVIDING EVERYONE'S NEEDS. GIVING THE ABILITY TO EVERYONE TO BECOME WHOLE. THE GREED OF MONEY BEING REVEALED. ALLOWING EVERYONE TO LIVE A MEANINGFUL EXISTENCE.

Prior to going to Afghanistan, I told my dad I wanted to open a church that had a school, nursery, homeless outreach program, gardens on the property, and clones and seeds for endless amounts of fruits, vegetables, and trees. Members will even have gardens at home. The church would purchase livestock and chickens. Everyone would share their skills with members of the congregation, allow knowledge to be spread amongst each other and a bunch of other stuff… But heaven?

WHEN WILL YOU ACCEPT MY WILL?

At this point, for the rest of the drive to Aspen, I really started contemplating everything I'd ever known. How is it that my spirit is telling me this? I know I can't be the first one who came to these conclusions. If it was this simple, why has no one come before me and just told me the truth?

YOU REMEMBER WHEN YOUR MOM TOLD YOU, "WELL, RYAN, IF YOU DON'T LIKE WHAT THEY ARE DOING, BE THE CHANGE." LET'S SAY YOU WILL MAKE YOUR MAMA PROUD.

I can accept that.

How will I, of all people, be able to convince the world of something no man has been able to convince them of doing before?

ARE YOU A MAN? REVEAL TO THEM THAT THEY ARE ENERGY, AND PROFESS IT BOLDLY, FOR THEY ARE MY CHILDREN AS WELL.

I accept the task. What to tell them?

THE SAME THING YOUR BROTHER TOLD YOU.

In the beginning of this book, Matthew 6 was presented to you. These are revelations Our Father gave me to give you all. First, to be better able to accept the truths in the book to come, let me lay down some simple foundations. First, we must understand science, because science is the systematic study of the structure and behavior of the physical and natural world through observation and experiment. In general, a scientific law is the description of an observed phenomenon. It doesn't explain why the phenomenon exists, or what causes it. The explanation of a phenomenon is called a scientific theory. Theory is something that man can come up with and recite over and over, but it still doesn't make it as strong as observations that never change and are accepted as scientific law.

In all the experimentation and studying, one of the laws scientists have determined is that energy cannot be created or destroyed. Science has also proved that our bodies move off electrical impulses. Because our bodies move off electrical impulses, we must accept that energy has to be inside of us. Our brains and hearts are in control of our energy. The heart sends out pulses, and the brain filters the energy from our heart to perform all the functions the body needs.

We are all made from dust. However, the energy inside our body is our soul, and it belongs to Our Father. Jesus gave us instruction on how to pray, but it isn't until we slow down and actually listen to what we are saying, can we even realize who we are praying to and what we are praying for. Those times in life, we may have felt we were telling a white lie, when we told others we were keeping them in our prayers. Most of the time we were telling the truth. We were just ignorant of why. The Lord's Prayer covers all believers.

Our Father which art in heaven.

Realize that Jesus said, "Our Father." He didn't say, "God." Furthermore, He gave us the same honor as Himself. He didn't claim Our Father to Himself. The second thing we must realize is that Our Father is not of this world. Our Father gave the world over to us to develop, so no one of his own accord can ever claim to be our leader. Our Father, however, left us with a guide to lead us. That guide is a piece and extension of Him, the Holy Spirit, which is Our Father's Spirit. He has never left nor forsaken us. We all have a little piece of Him inside us.

Hallowed be thy name.

Honor as holy. Our Father is good enough. If we don't call our physical parents by their first name, how then should we feel comfortable with call God, our Spiritual Father by His? Also His holiness applies to His Spirit as well. We do this all the time by referring to the Holy Spirit as our conscience. Once we rob the Holy Spirit of His trueness, the only thing left is a fragment of what could be. We pray to Our Father; however, we argue and debate His answers by not understanding and valuing the Holy Spirit as Our Father Himself inside us. We can easily see, by viewing God's Spirit as our conscience, we can never elevate Our Father to His proper level in our thinking. By viewing Our Father's Spirit as our conscience, we take ownership over Our Father, as opposed to honoring Him.

Thy kingdom come, thy will be done in Earth as it is in heaven.

The only way for Our Father's Kingdom to come is for us to realize that all of us are already in His Kingdom. The Earth itself is encompassed and surrounded by the heavens. The fact you have life means that the Creator decided to create you. To have life is the greatest gift to us all. Honoring Our Father automatically restores His Kingdom. The Kingdom of God is the same as the Body of Christ. The Church must do the work required for The Kingdom/Body of Christ to stand, with all of us working together and operating as one to serve Our Father's will. When we accept that His will is to be done in Earth as it is in Heaven, we can finally conclude that Heaven and Earth should match. When we perform Our Father's will on Earth as it is in Heaven, the two should and will be the same.

Scripture explains how the Earth is inside of Heaven.

Genesis 1:

> **6)** And God said, Let there be a firmament in the midst of the waters, and let it divide the waters from the waters. **7)** And God made the firmament and divided the waters which were under the firmament from the waters which were above the firmament: and it was so. **8)** And God called the firmament Heaven. And the evening and the morning were the second day. **9)** And God said, Let the waters under the heavens be gathered together unto one place, and let the dry land appear: and it was so. **10)** And God called the dry land Earth; and the gathering together of the waters called the Seas: and God saw that it was good."

This text should allow us to see that Earth is already inside of Heaven. The firmament itself is Heaven. The waters were separated by air. The air inside the bubble still contained water and land, but the water encased the land. Our Father separated the waters beneath Heaven, created dry land, and called it Earth. We are looking to get to Heaven when the air itself, our atmosphere, is Heaven. Heaven allows for the Earth to exist.

We are chasing and running to get to where we already are. Everything is based on perception. We are already in outer space. It is all relative to where you think you already exist. Second, we always wonder if our name will be in the Book of Life. We need to be fearful that our name will be stricken out of it. Furthermore, we should all be aware of the story we are telling, by simply living out our lives. From our story, we will all be judged. It isn't something for us to achieve; it is something we are constantly falling from. We continually fall from grace until we finally accept it. We do not elevate ourselves to grace. It is something being offered to us. The devil comes to rob, steal, and destroy. Understand, his entire purpose is to rob us of who we are, to steal our joy and to destroy us when we act in weakness. The devil's entire job is to constantly put us in a trap of feeling unworthy.

Give us this day our daily bread.

Everything coming from Our Father lasts only a day. Even when He was feeding us manna, it was only for a day. The energy Our Father gives us is only for that day. Anytime the children stranded in the desert tried to take extra manna, it would spoil and become rotten the next day. Too often, we try to use today's energy for tomorrow, as if we could bank today's energy or preserve it somehow for a later day.

When we are operating and doing things correctly, each day builds on the other. We have all these tasks our Spirit is telling us to do. However, we choose to spend the time and energy of that day thinking of something else. When we focus our time, energy and effort on today, we will automatically create a better tomorrow. The past weighs you down, and the future tries to speed you up. Our Father is trying to keep us balanced and in the sweet spot. Furthermore, to focus on the past and/or future creates stress and worries; both go against the will of Our Father.

Forgive us our debts as we forgive our debtors.

This automatically makes things in our lives, *give-and-take*. Furthermore, it exposes everything as a plural. We all must do these things, in order for the Body of Christ to stand, and the Kingdom of God to be revealed. The only way the Body can stand is for us to love each other unconditionally and without limits.

The Bible tells us that if we are to judge, we are to give righteous judgment. Christ our Savior is our example to follow. When He judged, He showed love. He healed others from their sinful state and instructed them to sin not, once they were healed. The only way to forgive others who trespass against us is to not keep a record of wrong.

- If we want Our Father to not keep a record of our wrongs, we must not keep a record of the wrongs of others.

- If we want to be forgiven by Our Father, we must forgive those who wronged us.
- If we want to know we are forgiven ahead of time, we must be willing to forgive others ahead of time.

The give and take portion of the prayer allows us to see the results in our lives, as we release them to others. The only way you will ever feel truly forgiven is to forgive others. The ability to forgive is God-given. To hold onto a grudge is a trait of the devil (us/our carnal mind), not of Our Spiritual Father, God, the Creator. We are the avatars that are groaning and complaining, instead of performing the Will of Our Father without exception.

Lead us not into temptation but deliver us from evil.

We must understand and accept when we are tempted, we have tempted ourselves. If Our Father commanded us not to be a stumbling block to others, why would we think He would be a stumbling block to us ? James Chapter 1 tried to get us to understand temptation. For us to be tempted, the carnal man has to be present. This is why James stated that trials and tribulations come to make you stronger and to count it as joy when they do come.

When Our Father reveals our carnality to us, we should count it as joy. Why? Because, once our carnality is revealed, we can rebuke it and repent (stop/have a change of heart). The more Our Father reveals ourselves to us; the more we can repent of the things within us that are unlike Him. If Our Father is leading us away from temptation, the only thing left to understand and accept is we ourselves are following after the devil. The lust of our own eye is leading us towards our death. Our carnality belongs to the devil. There is no way around our carnality but to die to ourselves, by removing our own feelings and emotions from Our Father's thinking. We are linked to evil simply by being born into our flesh, but we all must realize, we must operate from the Holy Spirit inside of us.

For thine is the Kingdom, the power, and the glory, forever and ever, amen.

Only Our Father is Our Father. No man can take credit for His works and deeds. We must restore honor and glory to Our Father. We must stop trying to take credit for the things He is doing and stop giving glory and honor to anyone or anything except the Creator. It is not by our might; it is not by our power. It is by His Spirit, the LORD of Hosts' will be done. The host must become host once more.

We must understand the principle of being a vessel and a temple. We can only be blessed to house Our Father. We house Our Father by allowing His Spirit, the Holy Spirit, to lead us. We become Christlike. God is fully in control of us, and His Kingdom is returned to Him. We fulfill our role as Christians by becoming Christlike, and we earn the title by admitting, we cannot add or take away from the Holy Spirit. We can only be vessels to and for it, adding to His glory but never taking away from it.

What is occurring today is we are robbing ourselves of our blessings by being disobedient. We robbed ourselves of the favor following Our Father gives us. Our Father will be praised, worshiped and honored, regardless of what we do, but we must perform Our Father's will for Him to return and be released on Earth. Our actions and beliefs must release Him, by our actions aligning with His will.

Our Father's Kingdom

I started thinking of everyone I knew. I thought of all my friends and associates who had acquired certain skills and knowledge. I thought of multiple family members and lifelong friends. I thought of everyone whom I felt Our Father had put into my life to perform His will. As I continued to go down the list in my head…

WHAT MAKES YOU THINK THIS IS MY LIST?

…I quickly understood the error in my thinking. My Father's Kingdom is to be built and designed by Him and Him alone. He doesn't need my thinking; He needs my obedience. He needs me always behind and being led by Him. I quickly thought of the chosen people. I thought of my ancestors. I thought of my lineage.

I realized that my human lineage had nothing to do with my Spiritual lineage. My Spiritual lineage is straight and to the point, Father-son, no more and no less. I then realized it is those who are of my Father's lineage who truly matter anyway. Our Father's Kingdom isn't dependent on race, religion or creed. It is dependent on whether a person believes in the Holy Spirit and performs love or not. The qualification to be a part of Our Father's Kingdom is whether you are loving or not. Even Jesus said, speak against the son of man and, it will be forgiven. However, speak a word against the Holy Ghost, and it shall not be forgiven.

What some could see as an abuse of love, others see as the performance of love. I can shine a negative light, or positive light on God's work. Our

Father says, "Let not your good be evil spoken." For someone to abuse love, someone else must have shown love. Whenever I think of someone taking advantage of another, I have to see the act of love performed on the "abuser." I had to admit. When I saw the abuse of love, I first had to see the act of love being performed. I failed to see all the examples that were being set because of my thinking. Due to the essence of love, it is easy to see the abuse of it. Due to the abuse of love, it makes others not want to perform love. Those performing love view it as an act of kindness and wish blessings upon you.

I thought of the people I borrowed money from, for the start-up of everything. I just knew for sure that I would easily pay them back and give them a little extra for helping me along my way. Instead, I am looking at the debt I now have, and feeling stress of my own accord because of not paying those people back by now. Not one of them has asked for repayment, but in my life, all the time, I've been lacking in finances. The devil is waiting to recall all the money I have lent out and was never repaid.

IT'S GIVE AND TAKE. YOU FEEL STRESS BECAUSE OF YOUR OWN THINKING. LOVE RELIEVES YOU OF THE PRESSURE, NOT THE RESPONSIBILITY.

I just want to be able to pay them back right now.

YOUR OWN JUDGMENT IS THE REASON YOU FEEL GUILT.

Yes, but I am not used to being indebted to anyone.

YOU AREN'T. YOU ARE INDEBTED TO LOVE.

I know, but it isn't You I owe money to.

JUST THINK OF ALL THE PEOPLE WHO HAVE BECOME INDEBTED TO YOU IN THE WORLD. YOU CAN'T EVEN REMEMBER THEM.

Yeah, but the world isn't as forgiving as me. They don't care what hardships I may have encountered.

BE HAPPY IT WAS MY LOVE THAT HELPED YOU AND NOT THE WORLD. DID YOU LEARN YOUR LESSON?

I learned, you provide me with the necessities I need. I learned, if I have to go too far out of my way, it is too far out of my way. I learned to be resourceful and to never focus on one thing so much, I allow a thousand other things to go wrong.

WHAT ABOUT THE TIMES YOU HAD THE MONEY TO PAY OTHERS BACK? DON'T HOLD BACK.

I learned that when You give me the things required for my life to become whole, to make it whole. If I pay back people when I first can, the stress of it taking longer than I wanted would never exist. I learned, the peace in favor is worth more than anything the world has to offer in the form of money. I learned Your Kingdom is already paid for.

By the act being done in love, it was deeper than family loaning me money. With love, loans are investments into your future. It is disappointing to all involved, when the future doesn't go as planned. My intentions were good natured. However, when they didn't pan out, the spirit in me was revealed. Did I strive to pay back my debts as quickly as possible? Did I tell myself that they got it, and they are okay? I was only delaying the inevitability of paying them back.

In life, I have learned to do things inside the Holy Spirit. The Holy Spirit will only allow me to take on a little. The Holy Spirit is cautious, and not greedy. The Holy Spirit is sober-minded. Sober-minded isn't meant to be taken as drunkenness or having a mind that's altered by the use of drugs and/or alcohol. The sober mind the Bible speaks of is to not look at myself from a high and mighty point of view. It is a moderate estimate, not one that stretches or pushes limits. To think soberly means to not allow vanity, pride, and ego to enter my mind.

I realized it was my Father who put people into my life to stop me from leaving Him. It is also my Father who puts me in contact with the right people to manifest His vision. The only way to build my Father's Kingdom is to stop trying to build up my own.

For us to build up Our Father's Kingdom, we have to first admit and see the difference in us creating ours. Jesus/Yeshua/Yahshua/ Yehoshua/ Yahushua consistently pointed to Our Father as His source. He never tried to take credit for what Our Father was doing. He is quoted saying, "Your will be done." If our Savior Himself can say, "Nevertheless not my will but thine be done," we all have to realize our misalignment.

For Our Father's will to be done, we must first eliminate our own will. This can be very hard to do. Our entire lives, we have been taught to plan, execute and develop more plans, for when we reach that level of life. With that being said, we must tackle our own freewill.

Freewill isn't as luxurious as many have made it out to be. It was once a beautiful thing; it was beautiful when nothing we thought of would be outside of Our Father's will. However, it was cursed, and now, it isn't anything to be glorified.

Our downfall was a trick of the enemy. We became tainted. Our Father had no choice but to cut us off from eternity out of love. He knew we all lacked the proper understanding at that point, but we could grow into what we needed to become. Once freewill was corrupted, laziness, procrastination, doubt, fear, anxiety, nervousness, greed, lust, deceit, pride, ego, and everything else were released.

- Freewill gives us the ability to journey into the wilderness by ourselves, with no guide.
- Freewill is how we occupy space that is meant for Our Father alone.
- Freewill is how the devil gains control over our thinking.

If freewill to go against Our Father didn't exist, perfection would automatically exist. Once we encompass this thought process, the Holy

Spirit can start to encompass us. The truth of what to do next becomes simple: Our Father's will. We would understand, it isn't us doing anything, but Our Father working through us doing everything. "What would Jesus do?" becomes, "What would I do?" He and we are one and the same, because we both embody Our Father's Spirit. To embody Our Father's Spirit is to allow Him to fully control and access us. To possess Our Father's Spirit isn't something we pull down, but something we kneel and bow down to. We can all kneel and listen.

Some may still ask, "Listen to what?" Our inner voice. The narrator of our life. The one who holds all our memories and dreams, both the ones we want to forget and the ones we hold so near and dear to our heart. Understand who and what the Holy Spirit is. The Holy Spirit knows all of our wrongs but never brings one negative emotion to them; He only brings the truth at all times. What we do with the truth is up to us. We have…

- hidden it,
- denied it,
- lied to ourselves about it,
- covered it up,
- changed from it,
- evolved from it, and
- distracted ourselves from it.

What we must admit is, we can't change it.

We have to allow the truth to reappear and humble us when and where it needs to, and to exalt us when and where we are following after it. The difference in the feelings and emotions we get from the truth the Holy Spirit gives us depends on what side of the truth we happen to be on. All of us are already born with ultimate truth. We instinctively know what the best possible thing we could do would be. However, due to our own foolishness and carnality, we aren't in a position to provide true love and help. By not being in that position, we can easily fall into the trap of feeling defeated before we even begin.

From us believing, a message from God comes from a certain cookie-cutter image. We have forgotten Our Father's warning He gave us. We must forget the versions of truth man has given us. We were instructed to not give credit to anyone due to their outer appearance or stature, whether it was social, economic, political, business-related, or as simple as how a person presents himself. Whatever pre-established judgment we have of anyone is sin and prejudice; to have something already in mind based upon someone's appearance is a flawed way of thinking. None of our judgment can be involved.

James 2:

> **1)** My brethren, have not the faith of our Lord Jesus Christ, the Lord of glory, with respect of persons. **2)** For if there come unto your assembly a man with a gold ring, in goodly apparel, and there come in also a poor man in vile raiment; **3)** And ye have respect to him that weareth the gay clothing, and say unto him, Sit thou here in a good place; and say to the poor, Stand thou there, or sit here under my footstool; **4)** Are ye not then partial in yourselves, and are become judges of evil thoughts? **5)** Hearken, my beloved brethren, Hath not God chosen the poor of this world rich in faith, and heirs of the kingdom which he hath promised to them that love him?**6)** But ye have despised the poor. Do not rich men oppress you and draw you before the judgment seats?

This text is letting us know that being swayed because of outer appearance is wrong. Not only that, but by believing in this manner, we allow the rich to oppress us and judge us, for things they are far more guilty of. To have a system designed for people to want themselves to be praised and glorified is wrong, therefore it is in error and sinful. We ought to perceive everyone as great. To deny one person greatness is to deny every one greatness.

To deny one person greatness is to deny every one greatness.

We are all capable of amazing things, based upon our interests, tools, and assets the Holy Spirit has given us. The things that interest us are the things that bring us the most joy. Just because our interest doesn't match another's, we shouldn't feel alarmed. This is the natural course of life. The Body of Christ has many members.

Allow the many members and parts to perform their purposes. Smarts and intelligence are based on the interests a person has. To hold a person high or low, based on their interests, makes us their judge and the jury. If Our Father saw fit, to make a person interested in being a street sweeper, who are we to judge him or her for serving that purpose? Furthermore, who are we to look down on someone who is serving the community in a positive nature? The love of money is known to be the root of all evil. However, most will never admit they love money.

In order to build Our Father's Kingdom, we must develop Our Father's interest. We have to stop spending our money on worldly possessions that amount to nothing and start the process of becoming the head once again. We must end the thought process of equating our resources to money and adapt to the thinking of adding resources by using our money. We forget that the rich/wealthy men of the Bible took their money and went after more possessions.

They didn't worry about money. They had gold and silver in abundance. To chase after money would have been frivolous and pointless to them. They already had the resources that money was and is intended to represent. Our Father's way amounts to the possession of resources, not acquiring more money. When we accept, the concept of resources over money. We then understand the things of the Spirit. When we conclude, the resources Our Father gives us are our provisions, which no man is supposed to control. We are ready to perform His will.

Matthew 22:

> **17)** Tell us therefore, What thinkest thou? Is it lawful to give tribute unto Caesar, or not? **18)** But Jesus perceived their wickedness, and said, Why tempt ye

me, ye hypocrites? **19)** Shew me the tribute money. And they brought unto him a penny. **20)** And he saith unto them, Whose is this image and superscription? **21)** They say unto him, Caesar's. Then saith he unto them, Render therefore unto Caesar the things which are Caesar's; and unto God the things that are God's.

Mark 12:

14) And when they were come, they say unto him, Master, we know that thou art true, and carest for no man: for thou regardest not the person of men, but teachest the way of God in truth: Is it lawful to give tribute to Caesar, or not? **15)** Shall we give, or shall we not give? But he, knowing their hypocrisy, said unto them, Why tempt ye me? bring me a penny, that I may see it. **16)** And they brought it. And he saith unto them, Whose is this image and superscription? And they said unto him, Caesar's. **17)** And Jesus answering said unto them, Render to Caesar the things that are Caesar's, and to God the things that are God's. And they marveled at him.

Luke 20:

And they asked him, saying, Master, we know that thou sayest and teachest rightly, neither acceptest thou the person of any, but teachest the way of God truly: **22)** Is it lawful for us to give tribute unto Caesar, or no? **23)** But he perceived their craftiness, and said unto them, Why tempt ye me? **24)** Shew me a penny. Whose image and superscription hath it? They answered and said, Caesar's. **25)** And he said unto them, Render therefore unto Caesar the things which be Caesar's, and unto God the things which be God's. **26)** And they could not take hold of his words before the people: and they marveled at his answer and held their peace.

This important lesson appears in three of the four Gospels, but what is most overlooked is that which is right in front of our faces. Jesus asked whose image and superscription the coin had. He then followed by saying, give to Caesar what is Caesar's. The deeper meaning and most overlooked fact was the inscription made the coin belong to Caesar. Therefore, all money stamped by Caesar was for Caesar. We expand on it and realize, money without resources is nothing. Jesus then followed, unto God the things that are God's. The plot thickens and gets deeper. Not only are we to return the resources to God, but we must also return ourselves to God.

Money does both. It strips individuals of resources. Furthermore, it enslaves us all to it. As long as money is number one, everything else is beneath it. Money then determines the cost/worth of everything, thereby disrupting the natural balance of every member of the Body, and our intended purpose of helping each other. Money dictates value and stature. Morals and values go out the window, and Our Father's Kingdom can never be built. The Body of Christ standing means all of man's attempts to control others will fail and fall.

Our Father's Kingdom is a network based on love and empowering one another. To establish Our Father's Kingdom, we must reestablish Our Father's principles over our own. To be successful must become more than how much money a person has, or what net worth he or she has acquired. In Our Father's Kingdom, a good or bad day is judged on how much love we shared, spread, and gave that day. We must change our perception from basing good or bad on the amount of money acquired or made, to how in tune we were with Our Father's Spirit on any given day. Once we start working towards love, all these things we need will naturally be added.

Labor in Love

Matthew 9:

35) And Jesus went about all the cities and villages, teaching in their synagogues, and preaching the gospel of the kingdom, and healing every sickness and every disease among the people. **36)** But when he saw the multitudes, he was moved with compassion on them, because they fainted, and were scattered abroad, as sheep having no shepherd. **37)** Then saith he unto his disciples, The harvest truly is plenteous, but the labourers are few; **38)** Pray ye therefore the Lord of the harvest, that he will send forth labourers into his harvest.

Luke 10:

2) Therefore said he unto them, The harvest truly is great, but the labourers are few: pray ye therefore the Lord of the harvest, that he would send forth labourers into his harvest. **3)** Go your ways: behold, I send you forth as lambs among wolves. **4)** Carry neither purse, nor scrip, nor shoes: and salute no man by the way. **5)** And into whatsoever house ye enter, first say, Peace be to this house. **6)** And if the son of peace be there, your peace shall rest upon it: if not, it shall turn to you again. **7)** And in the same house remain, eating and drinking such things as they give: for the labourer is worthy of his hire. Go not from house to house. **8)** And into whatsoever city ye enter, and they receive you, eat such things as are set before you: **9)** And heal the sick that are therein, and say unto them, the kingdom of God is come nigh unto you. **10)** But into whatsoever city ye enter, and they receive you not, go your ways out into the streets of the same, and say, **11)** Even the very dust of your city, which cleaveth on us, we do wipe off against you: notwithstanding be ye sure of this, that the kingdom of God is come nigh unto you.

In all of my learning, I've realized I am just a laborer. I learned what I once thought was so special to attain was simply for me to do the things I already knew. Planting seeds of life came naturally for me. Encouraging someone is as simple as saying, "You can do it." The seed is now planted. When someone comes back with a simple, "You got this," those are all the words needed for the transition from one behavior to another to be completed and cemented in someone's mind. I had given seeds and water freely to people throughout my whole life, then I had to apologize and repent for sowing other seeds in others' minds.

To give thought to a possibility is limited to what my faith (beliefs) allows. I knew I could either sprout a seed my Father gave me and give it life or abandon the thought and let it die. It is all dependent on where I focus my time, energy, and effort. As long as I paid attention, I could do anything in life. I also knew to never allow myself to get boastful enough to think I was better than another. Therefore, to tell another to shoot for their dreams was easy for me. Taking the time to hear another's dreams is one of the most loving things we can do. To sit and entertain someone every time they are willing to dream, can only be done in love.

I understand the need of going the extra mile and asking someone where they are on their journey. I understand checking up and doing follow-ups and offering words of encouragement is planting more seeds and giving more water. I also realize the seeds I planted in others resulted in them planting those same seeds in others. Gathering up Our Father's harvest can only be done, if I have sown seeds of love, not discord, in another's life. When any of my friends are angry, I know I could stand in front of them, firmly look them in the eye, and say, "Chill out," and vice versa. The number of people who attend church houses shows just a small example of how many are truly yearning to learn of Our Father. There are plenty of people wanting to hear the message of Our Father. Until I submit myself to perform His will, I am robbing others of experiencing the Holy Spirit.

MY YOKE IS EASY AND MY BURDEN IS LIGHT.

You're really telling me it is that simple and easy?

THE SERPENT DECEIVED EVE THROUGH HIS CRAFTINESS IN USING FALSE INFORMATION. HIS ENTIRE PURPOSE IS TO STEER PEOPLE'S MINDS FROM THE TRUE SIMPLICITY, SINGLENESS, SINCERITY OF MENTAL HONESTY THAT IS IN CHRIST.

I knew "make it simple, it is simple, make it hard, it is hard" was the way to go.

MAKING EVERYTHING SIMPLE IS HOW YOU REACH PEACE IN ANYTHING. YOU KNOW WHAT TO DO. YOU HAVE TO ACCEPT DOING IT.

I can never allow my feelings and emotions to get in Your way of laboring in love.

The seeds and water that I give to others is the knowledge of the Holy Spirit. The more seeds and water I plant and give freely, the more Our Father's Spirit can grow freely in others. He gives the increase to everyone in their own time. I had mistakenly, but understandably waited for the right time, the right moment, the right following, the right words, the moment the stars, moons, planets and suns aligned. Our Father revealed to me there is no such alignment. His will has already been set forth and explained to us.

I had to bear my own cross and pick up His work. I could say to myself, All I want, "If I was here or there, if I had this sect of people or that sect of people's attention, if I build up my followers on social media and so forth and so on, things would be different and easier." However, no matter the road or path Our Father has put me on, the only thing I could really do is walk in His Spirit. I had to learn to stop waiting and overthinking, and instead, listen and perform.

I had to learn, if my words were not accepted, to simply dust off my feet like it says in Luke 10. I had to learn the hard way that not everyone is interested in Our Father's Spirit. Many are called, few are chosen. I learned I had to stop just hearing the calling and start walking in my true purpose and calling. I learned the glue that is love was and is still there; love is as adhesive as it has ever been. However, I then realized, dried glue on an envelope serves no purpose, until moisture is applied. The glue that is meant to hold us together is there. It is up to us to water and nurture it into its proper purpose.

If a new secretary comes along and starts stapling the envelopes, yes, a seal is created, but it isn't as good as the seal the glue would have created. Just because there is more than one way to tackle and handle a situation doesn't mean each way is equally effective. Until I was ready to be efficient and effective, any way a task could be completed would have forever been good enough. It was not until I wanted to be perfected, that I stopped doing things any kind of way that no longer served a purpose towards perfection.

I learned, for Our Father's kingdom to be built, I had to become His friend and help Him. I help Him by becoming one of His laborers. The growth comes from Our Father. A laborer can only plant, water, and harvest. Our Father's Kingdom is built through spreading love and encouraging others to live up to their fullest potential. The main thing preventing me from carrying out Our Father's will was believing I could be part of the world and continuing to rely on my own thinking.

THERE IS NEVER A REASON TO THINK WHEN YOU ARE FOLLOWING AFTER ME.

As soon as we allow ourselves to think, we must accept that we have also allowed ourselves to become foolish. It is always foolish to lean on our own understanding, when Our Father's thinking is there for us, instead. By trying to develop and perfect our own thinking, we continue to fall short of what Our Father is trying to give us. Our overall impatience prevents us from achieving our end goal. Furthermore, when we judge, the process is based upon our limited understanding, we are preventing the development and growth Our Father requires of us Spiritually.

If we were about Our Father's business, it would be a joy to encounter someone negative. We would automatically see and view it as an opportunity to show and spread love. The most powerful thing about love is what most people overlook. Love overtakes any other emotion out there and replaces it with itself. God's love is the only thing out there that can literally absorb and consume every other emotion known to man. Our Father's love releases an immeasurable amount of joy. The feeling we receive when doing Our Father's will far surpass that of any other. To see someone's growth and maturity is one of the biggest blessings of them all, but we need to remember, to whom much is given, much is required. Our own shortcomings are what prevent us from doing Our Father's will completely.

Due to our own expectations of what we feel and think growth should and could be, we minimize the work Our Father is doing. To build on a little is how we get to a lot. A great many people have been tricked to abandon the foundation and shoot for the stars. Then, in turn, they are left to wonder why everything they tried to build up always falls and crumbles. Our job and goal are to accept that adding another to the Body of Christ is the most productive thing we could do on any given day. To transform someone's mind into operating with a proper thought process serves the community far more than a handout of any sort. To get people in tune with the Holy Spirit inside of them is to unlock unlimited potential in their life. Therefore, the spreading of the good news and the gospel must become our focal point.

Many may feel this is already happening, but if someone came out blatantly, bluntly, and boldly saying, "We are all a part of Jesus's body, therefore once we have accepted Our Father's Spirit as our own, we too are now an extension of Our Father. Through the adoption of the Holy Spirit, we allow Our Father's Spirit to dwell inside us. The Holy Spirit flows through us just like it did through Jesus," the immediate reaction by most would be saying, "That is blasphemous," which was the same reaction given to Jesus. We are to believe as Jesus believed. Therefore, to rob someone of the true knowledge of why they are called brother and sister is to rob them of the good news and the true gospel. Jesus' messages and teachings need to be understood and accepted in our lives. Blind faith is blind. Many walk in darkness because the Holy Spirit is being robbed of His truth and limelight.

We are to believe as Jesus believed. Therefore, to rob someone of the true knowledge of why they are called brother and sister, is to rob them of the good news and the true gospel.

The same Father, Son (Daughter/Child) and Holy Spirit Trinity is you, as well as it is me. We can all choose to have Our Father's Spirit inside of ourselves. It is easy and simple to see which one to choose when the facts are presented simply and are easy to understand. This is the good news and gospel we are supposed to spread and preach. We can become sons and daughters to Our Father by allowing Him to flow through us.

To baptize another in the Spirit is to reveal the Holy Spirit in others, to others. Then and only then can we be many members in one body. The Body of Christ is united via the Holy Spirit. The only way to tap into the Holy Spirit is by adopting Our Father's Spirit of charity. Charity is giving unconditional and unlimited love to the deserving and undeserving. We are instructed to give to the poor. We are never supposed to take advantage of the state another brother or sister is in. We are commanded to love our brother as Our Father Himself loves us. The world chooses to exploit people's lack of knowledge. God has already told us, greater is He that is inside me than He that is in the world.

With that being said, the application of unconditional and unlimited love is charity. Love is an action. Love is something to do and carry out; charity is love done in perfection. Charity encompasses the very thing love is meant to represent, grace and mercy being a gateway to favor. Grace and mercy are how we can spread Our Father's will to all. It is what gives us the ability to tap into unlimited and unconditional love. Charity's meaning has been manipulated to take away from its true purpose relating to love. Charity is the free giving away of love to anyone in need; charity is not donating money. We all know everyone needs love, so charity is how we are able to fulfill this need. Many say that this is an impossible task. However, Paul already gave us the way:

1 Corinthians 13:

> 4) Charity suffereth long, and is kind; charity envieth not; charity vaunteth not itself, is not puffed up, 5) Doth not behave itself unseemly, seeketh not her own, is not easily provoked, thinketh no evil; 6) Rejoiceth not in iniquity, but rejoiceth in the truth; 7) Beareth all things, believeth all things, hopeth all things, endureth all things. 8) Charity never faileth: but whether there be prophecies, they shall fail; whether there be tongues, they shall cease; whether there be knowledge, it shall vanish away. 9) For we know in part, and we prophesy in part. 10) But when that which is perfect is come, then that which is in part shall be done away. 11) When I was a child, I spake as a child, I understood as a child, I thought as a child: but when I became a man, I put away childish things. 12) For now we see through a glass, darkly; but then face to face: now I know in part; but then shall I know even as I am known. 13) And now abideth faith, hope, charity, these three; but the greatest of these is charity.

Charity is the "no kidding" application of our Faith and Hope. Charity is allowing love to be the glue to the foundation Our Father is trying to build within us. Charity is how we access becoming full-time sowers and waterers of seeds. Many want to think that Our Father's army will come in this way or that way. However, the Body of Christ must be full of laborers in love.

To attack the devil head on, we must tackle carnality head on. We must attack the physical via spiritual warfare. It is through someone's thinking, we can get that person to change. We must stop targeting people's actions. Our Father instructs us to repent. In order to repent, we must change the way we think and look at things. As long as we look at things from a carnal standpoint, we will never see any reason to change. We will only recognize the world as imperfect; we will never consider perfecting it.

Laborers of love see the imperfections of the world and perform the task of creating Our Father's Kingdom. The only way to allow for the creation of Our Father's Kingdom is to allow the Holy Ghost to have His proper place. For thine is the Kingdom, power and the glory, forever and ever. To some people, it will be a brand new idea or a new way of looking at things. They will have to come to grips with something completely foreign to them. They will not have the proper understanding to receive everything we are saying. They will admit that it rings of truth, but they will not buy into it fully. As long as we practice patience and live in peace, the seed has soil for it to grow.

The Bible speaks of dusting off our feet to someone who doesn't receive our message. Instead of this being taken as a bitter act, or an act looked upon as disgracing another. Instead, look at it as the dust being the soil, the seed needs to grow. The dust is peace. Anytime we plant a seed in discord, it will never grow. It is our job as laborers in love to always allow peace to be upon us and with us. Once a person has received a seed, the same truth is now water for the seed to grow. The most important thing to remember is, Our Father gives the increase.

To give life and meaning to this process, we can look at it like teaching a kid how to read and write. In the beginning, it is a very tedious task, but after learning the alphabet and some common words, the child's vocabulary trampolines and catapults to a level we never thought they would reach in such a short time. The more basics we give, and the more concepts we break down for them. The more they know how to apply the information for themselves. We are to empower one another and trust that Our Father has complete control, and He will guide others just as He guides us.

The time has come for us to remove our trust in man and stop wondering why all men begin to abuse their power over time. All men are carnal, therefore anyone left unchecked by the Holy Spirit is destined to fail. It is only the Holy Spirit and Our Father who can take credit for the things of the Spirit. We never were to put our trust in man, but we were always taught to put our trust and faith in Our Father. We must trust the fact that our love is greater than all the hate and division the enemy highlights. In order to build Our Father's Kingdom, we must relinquish control back to Him. We must put our own thoughts to the side. We must follow the rules and guidelines He has already given and laid out for us. All we have to do is LOVE, as He has commanded us to do.

It is only the Spirit that can take credit for the Spirit.

The Greatest Love of All

God, I don't get it. I tried everything I know how. I know there is a way for Your will to be done on Earth. It is Your Son's prayer.

RYAN WHAT ARE YOU TALKING ABOUT NOW?

I have been trying to spread your message. I just don't get why they don't get it! I want the fullness of it all to be revealed in an instant. The gift of Your Spirit is the greatest gift of them all, and You giving us Your Son to teach us truly of Your ways. We now have no excuse as to man tainting you. Your Son had Your Spirit. By Your Son being obedient to You, we all received an unfiltered glimpse on You. So many today want to say that the Bible is tainted and corrupt. I understand completely the reasons why they feel like they do. The Bible is being taught in bits and pieces. People are using it to further their own agendas, and not Yours.

DID YOU EVER ASK ME WHAT TO SAY?

For what? I just let You flow through me. I am constantly in awe of the things I learn, as the words You give others flow out of my mouth.

EXACTLY! IT IS ME CONSTANTLY REACHING OUT, TRYING TO GET MY CHILDREN TO RETURN TO THE FULLNESS I WANT ALL OF THEM TO BE.

Well, how come, no matter what You say, no one seems to get it, like I know they should?

A PERSON CAN ONLY BELIEVE WHAT THEY CHOOSE TO BELIEVE. YOU THINK THAT IN THE SPREADING OF THE GOSPEL, IT WILL ALWAYS BE EASY BECAUSE YOU KNOW THE RESULTS OF TAKING ON THE GOSPEL. TO OTHERS IT SOUNDS LIKE FINGERNAILS BEING RUN ACROSS A CHALKBOARD. YOUR JOB IS TO PERFORM MY WILL. IT ISN'T YOUR JOB TO JUDGE OTHERS WHILE YOU PERFORM IT.

Judge? I have tried everything I know to become non-judgmental. I have even stopped trying to equate certain cars I see with the person driving them. I try to give Your love to others at all times. I am constantly pointing others to You. I constantly post about You on social media. I try to get others to understand the things You have shown me.

THE BIGGEST PROBLEM OF ALL, YOU HAVE ALLOWED THE DEVIL TO CONVINCE YOU THAT TRYING IS SOMETHING TO BE PROUD OF.

My whole life, I have been told to fight the good fight, to do the best that I can in life and to try hard at everything I do. I thought everything in life stemmed from someone trying.

IN LIFE, YOU DECIDED TO DO SOMETHING, AND IT WAS DONE.

STOP THINKING THERE IS MORE TO IT THAN THAT.

You say that like the devil doesn't present obstacles and battles along the way. I am constantly having to battle, day-to-day to hold on to you.

RYAN, WHY DO YOU FEEL YOU HAVE TO FIGHT A FIGHT THAT IS ALREADY WON?

I don't...

WELL, WHY DO YOU FEEL SO COMFORTABLE ENTERING AND EXITING MY SPIRIT? YOU ARE BACKSLIDING, AND IT IS AN OVERALL PATTERN OF BEING LUKEWARM.

I never looked at it like that.

I KNOW.

I get it now. Of all the things Jesus said and did, He always ended with, "…sin not." The second I return to thinking of myself as myself, I cut myself off from You. By me looking at myself as myself, I could never humble myself enough to repent and become a vessel for You.

MANY WANT TO BE A VESSEL FOR ME. FEW WANT TO REMAIN CONNECTED TO ME AT ALL TIMES.

Connecting at all times is hard. People are disrespectful and full of their pride and egos. It is hard to love the unlovable.

WHO IS UNLOVABLE?

The ones who refuse to repent! I am so tired of dealing with people who are stuck in their feelings. I am tired of dealing with naysayers.

SO, WHAT YOU ARE REALLY SAYING IS, YOU ARE TIRED OF SINNERS?

YES!!!! Why, Yes, I am.

WHO DID I SEND MY SON TO SAVE?

Sinners.

WHO WILL DID YOU DECIDE TO TAKE ON?

Yours.

WELL, HOW ARE YOU TIRED OF THE VERY THING I AM TRYING TO SAVE?

I love the sinner's soul. Their actions and sins are what aggravate me.

WELL, WHY ONCE YOU INTRODUCE OTHERS TO ME, DO YOU NEGLECT TO TELL THEM TO SIN NOT? HASN'T MY SON TOLD YOU ALL TO BE YE PERFECT AS YOUR FATHER IN HEAVEN IS PERFECT?

I know, but we have become convinced that on Earth we are all flesh, and by being flesh, we are all imperfect and all have fallen short of your glory.

JUST BECAUSE YOU ALL HAVE FALLEN SHORT, IT DOESN'T MEAN I DON'T GIVE THE INCREASE TO PERFECTION. I JUST WANT YOU ALL TO KNOW AND RECOGNIZE THAT I AM THE ONE WHO GIVES THE INCREASE. IT IS I WHO CAN PERFECT ALL THAT IS AMONGST YOU.

To give you an update on current events, there are a lot of people that feel as though you can be doing a better job. If you are all powerful and knowing, why don't you just make them submit? If you are real, why don't you make yourself known? Why is there hate? Why is there poverty? The list can go on and on.

WELL, IF THAT IS HOW THEY FEEL, THEY STILL HAVEN'T ACCEPTED WHAT I AM GIVING. DO I GIVE YOU PEACE?

Yes.

STRENGTH?

Yes.

COMFORT?

Yes.

LOVE? PATIENCE? ENDURANCE? HOPE? JOY? NEEDS? WANTS? DREAMS?

Yes.

IF I GIVE MYSELF FREELY TO YOU ALL, WHAT MORE CAN BE DONE THAN WHAT IS DONE? I GAVE YOU ALL FREEWILL. IF ANYONE MAKES THE CHOICE TO CONTINUE TO CHOOSE THEMSELVES OVER ME, THERE IS NOTHING I CAN DO.

I don't understand how someone can choose to be themselves over You.

YOU DO IT ALL THE TIME WITHOUT KNOWLEDGE OF IT. LET'S TRY THIS A DIFFERENT WAY. WHAT IS IT THAT SAVES YOU?

Your Spirit. In order for me to believe in Jesus, I must believe as Jesus. Being a disciple to Him automatically leads everything back to you.

IN ORDER FOR MY SPIRIT TO BE PRESENT IN YOU, WHAT DO YOU THINK MUST HAPPEN TO YOUR SPIRIT?

I have to get out of the way. My thoughts, thinking, judgments and reactions have to take a back seat to Yours.

WHEN HAVE YOU EVER KNOWN YOURSELF TO SHUT UP?

Never.

TRUST ME, I KNOW. OBVIOUSLY, YOU CAN'T GET OUT OF THE WAY IF YOU STILL THINK I NEED YOU.

I know you don't need me.

WHEN YOU ENTER INTO MY SPIRIT, WHAT DO YOU LEAVE BEHIND?

Me. My thoughts and thinking. I just accept doing what You want me to do.

WHENEVER YOU ARE FEELING DOWN AND OUT, OR ANY FORM OF EVIL, WHOSE THOUGHTS ARE PRESENT?

Mine.

HOW DO YOU GO FROM ENTERING INTO MY SPIRIT AND THINKING AND RETURNING TO YOURSELF WITHOUT NOTICING?

I don't know. It happens naturally. I have been me my entire life. I don't notice when I return. I think I am connected to You at all times; therefore, it is hard to notice when I appear in my mind.

I JUST TOLD YOU. EVERYTIME YOU FEEL NEGATIVITY, YOU ARE PRESENT.

Is it really that simple?

NO.

Well, give me complicated .

WHEN YOU ENTER INTO ME, YOU UNDERSTAND THAT YOU MUST THINK AND ACT LIKE ME. YOU ALLOW MY SPIRIT TO DWELL IN YOU. WHEN LIFE HAPPENS, YOU TAKE YOUR MIND OFF OF ME AND PUT IT ONTO WHAT IS HAPPENING IN THE MOMENT. IN THAT MOMENT, YOU ALLOW YOURSELF TO LOOK AT YOURSELF AS RYAN, AND NOT ME. WHEN YOU THINK OF YOURSELF AS RYAN, THE SAME ACTIONS THAT ARE DEEMED GREAT IN MY EYES ARE WEAK IN YOURS. YOU ALLOW MY GOOD TO BE SPOKEN BADLY OF ALL THE TIME. IN YOUR MOMENTS OF ANGER, FRUSTRATION AND

DISAPPOINTMENTS, YOU TAKE ON YOUR FLESH. YOU FAIL TO SEE THAT YOU HAVE ALLOWED SOMETHING TO SEPARATE YOU FROM ME.

I never want to be disconnected from You.

YOU MUST DIE IN ORDER FOR YOU TO REMAIN IN ME.

Die? That is a little extreme, don't You think?

YOUR EXISTENCE IS LOST IN ME. WHEN YOU ENTER MY SPIRIT, YOU TAKE ON MY SPIRIT. ONCE YOU TAKE ON MY SPIRIT, IT IS ONLY MY SPIRIT THAT CAN GET CREDIT FOR ANYTHING YOU PERFORM. YOU CAN NO LONGER VIEW YOURSELF DIFFERENTLY, IF YOU KEEP THINKING IT IS YOU PERFORMING MY WILL. IT IS ME PERFORMING MY WILL THROUGH YOU. YOU ARE THE VESSEL; I AM THE POTTER. I DECIDED THAT EVERY VESSEL SHOULD BE FILLED WITH LOVE. HOW DO YOU EXPECT TO BE MADE NEW, IF YOU KEEP VIEWING YOURSELF AS THE SAME? YOU ADMIT TO ME ALL THE TIME HOW HARD IT IS TO LOVE. I KEEP TELLING YOU MY YOKE IS EASY AND MY BURDENS ARE LIGHT.

I thought it was a transition, not death. No one ever told me I had to die in order to perform Your will.

HOW CAN YOU SAY THAT? MY SON AND YOUR BROTHER DID.

I don't remember reading that.

READ JOHN 15 AGAIN. IT IS YOUR JOB TO ACCEPT MY WORDS, NOT QUESTION THEM. IF I AM THE TRUTH AND THE LIGHT, ANY OF YOUR THOUGHTS AND THINKING LIMIT MY ABILITY TO FLOW THROUGH YOU. THE ONLY WAY FOR ME TO FLOW THROUGH YOU WITHOUT INTERFERENCE IS FOR YOUR THINKING TO BE NON-EXISTENT.

Ok. Let me make sure I understand this. You being the only bearer of good fruit (the vine), I can only join you in bearing good fruit (by becoming the branch). When I choose to think on my own and think I can perform good on my own, I automatically cut myself off from You and wither away. I can't do it without You.

WHAT ABOUT MY WORDS ABIDING IN YOU?

Your words are constantly being played out in my mind as a correction to my actions and thinking. In order for me to remain in You, Your words of correction must remain in me.

AND NOW FOR THE GOOD PART.

My wishes and Your wishes become the same . Anything I ask for shall be done unto me, because anything I ask is within your will. I will become extra fruitful and pleasing to You and become a true disciple of Jesus.

KEEP READING SO I CAN GIVE YOU THE COMPLETENESS OF IT ALL.

Love. I should have known it. You loved Jesus. Jesus loved us, and it is up to us to continue in Your love.

WHAT IS THE ONLY WAY TO LOVE?

The same way You loved Jesus and Jesus loved us...unconditionally and completely with no regard to person.

I DIDN'T ASK HOW YOU SHOULD LOVE. I ASKED, WHAT IS THE ONLY WAY TO LOVE?

To lay down my life.

WHY?

I will always get in Your way. I cannot take any credit for love. To remain constantly in You, I have to give up me. I am the one tied to the feelings and emotions of life. I have to die to my thinking, in order to always remain in Your love.

WHAT IS THE GREATEST LOVE OF ALL?

To lay down my life for my friends.

YOU NOW KNOW WHAT IT MEANS TO HAVE A FRIEND IN JESUS?

Yes. His teachings allowed me the path directly to You. Plus, He taught, shared, and enlightened others as opposed to keeping all of His knowledge to Himself.

WHAT ABOUT THE PERSECUTION AND HATRED THAT YOU WILL ENCOUNTER?

I get it. When anyone is stuck in their own thinking, explaining to them why they are wrong for it will always result in persecution and hatred unless they have Your Spirit. Furthermore, the truth will always be hated by the world, because this world wasn't built on the truth.

ONE LAST THING.

Ok.

WHEN YOU DIE TO SELF, WHAT SHOULD YOU BECOME?

You.

EXPLAIN?

I have to believe as Jesus believed. Jesus believed You flowed through Him because You did. I must join His beliefs by faith. In faith (my beliefs), there is hope to fuel me to become more like You. I understand, the only way to be like You is to abandon me.

HOW?

Jesus paid it all. All I have to do is have faith . You add the rest. You give me everything I need and supply all my needs. I know You give me access to You. Therefore, I have an unlimited supply of everything You offer. All I have to do is accept all of the good You have for me, and abandon all of the bad I have due to my own thinking and judgements.

SHOULD YOU ABANDON MY SPIRIT EVER AGAIN?

No! Thank You Father for everything.

THANK ME BY NOT ABANDONING ME AGAIN. NEVER VIEW YOURSELF AS YOURSELF AGAIN. ALWAYS CHOOSE TO BE ME. UNITE WITH YOUR BROTHERS AND SISTERS. IT IS POINTLESS TO KNOW ME AND NOT SERVE ME. HONOR ME BY BEING AN EXAMPLE OF ME. LOVE UNCONDITIONALLY BY BEING MY FRIEND. STAND AND WALK IN THE SPIRIT WITH ME.

What is next, LORD?

UNITE WITH AS MANY OF YOUR BROTHERS AND SISTERS AS YOU CAN, WHO HAS CHOSEN TO LAY DOWN THEIR LIVES AND ACCEPT THEIR WHITE ROBES. JUST MAKE SURE YOU ALWAYS WEAR YOURS, AND STOP TAKING IT OFF AND PUTTING IT ON. THE KINGDOM OF HEAVEN IS AT HAND. UNCONDITIONAL LOVE IS THE KEY TO UNLOCKING HEAVEN IN EARTH. MY WILL IN HEAVEN IS LOVE. MY WILL IS THE SAME ON EARTH AS IT IS IN HEAVEN. MY CHILDREN BELONG IN MY HOUSE. LOVE IS LOVE. I AM THAT I AM.

In all my attempts at introducing others to the Spirit, I never truly remained in the Spirit. I allowed my own thinking to rationalize and interact with others. Even with the knowledge, feelings and emotions are the devil's playground, I interacted with others based on their feelings and emotions. I realized there was only one way to eliminate feelings and emotions from the equation; I had to abandon my flesh and enter into the Spirit. I had to learn to be in the Spirit at all times, and to never abandon it for my flesh. In the Spirit and the Spirit alone, my pride, ego and vanity cannot exist. I must always unlock the true power within me, Our Father's Spirit, the Holy Spirit itself, waiting to be activated inside of me. This is the single way of life we all can agree on. Joy and peace that pass all understanding being released, and most of all, the power to eliminate hate with love.

We must all come to the acknowledgement of what power is inside of us. We are all connected to God and His Spirit. We must come to understand and accept that every action has an equal and opposite reaction. Every stroke of our egos is a strike on another's back. We must abandon thinking of life as individuals and start thinking of life as a group. There is only one way for those who dedicate their life to Our Father, to live. There is only one place for God's Children to dwell: His house and His house alone. We all know what love is and isn't. We all harbor emotions and feelings tied to a truth, or The Truth. We all must then understand that, for this exact reason, we must abandon feelings and emotions, and accept the ultimate Truth. The only truth those who believe in God can all agree on, is love. Love is how we strip the devil and the world of its power.

Once we accept love is the way, the only way for us all to interact with each other is love. We all judge others based on "moods and vibes," a person's "energy." The mood, vibe and energy we all look for is love. The more loving we can identify a person to be, the safer and more comfortable we feel around them. The "it feels like I have known him or her my entire life" level of friendship is attained. This connection is the only connection anyone who believes in Our Father should have. If we hold back our love, we automatically put a lampshade on the light that is inside of us all. We all must accept negative feelings and emotions are only felt or experienced when our pride and judgment are active. When someone says, they believe in God. The next question should be, "Do you know Him as Our Father?"

With all thy getting, get an understanding. Constantly, we have so much information thrown at us. We are bombarded with useless information all the time. The biggest scheme the devil has going for him is stealing attention away from God. Due to people wanting to be entertained so much, brainwashing has become easy. Most never realizing, we have been taught how to think and feel, when certain situations happen in life. We've been taught to want and crave certain things. Since our childhoods, the world has been programming us to feed into its programming and thinking. We have been taught to chase after vanity. We have been led our entire lives to our egos. We have been taught to think, to explore emotions as entertainment. The entire time, seeds are being planted; seeds to invoke certain feelings and emotions when certain events are experienced in life.

The highs and lows of life are pre-programmed based on our thinking. To be grateful to have life and enjoy our day costs nothing. We can have joy in any situation. This is how love endures. Being connected to love is how we unlock complete joy. Complete joy is unlimited happiness. A constant smile and a certain cheer that stands out to others. When we believe in God, we come to the knowledge of how we must act. This is why, in Romans, the law is explained as death. Death to all the actions our carnality wants to hold on to. The truth our carnality (our own thinking) does not want to accept is it isn't needed. Furthermore, Our Father does not want it. It is the division between Him and us. Our carnality is what we all must lay down, in order to take on His will for us.

It is only when we take on Our Father's will, do we become His Children. In order to be His Child, we must accept His Spirit and get rid of ours. It is only then that greed, lust, envy, and all of the evil of the world can be overcome. We are more than overcomers. We are all experiencing life. It is up to us all to live the life Our Father tells us to live. We can allow other gods and idols to take His place, or we can stay true to His word and worship and honor only Him. To do that, we all must admit, anything that takes away from us identifying as Him is a distraction and trap of the devil. The devil can only influence our egos. God Our Father has always had control of our souls. We have to return to the truth of our souls and reject the truth of our flesh. The truth of our souls is we belong to Our Father and to Our Father alone.

The only problem with understanding is thinking it is a choice, or an option to perform love. The real truth is we are commanded to love. We who believe in God must accept that in order to believe in God, our actions must match His Spirit. Galatians Chapter 5 explains the fruit of the Spirit versus the fruit of the flesh. We must all accept. Once we believe as Jesus believed, we all must see ourselves as God's Spirit and not our flesh.

We must all accept. Once we believe as Jesus believed, we all must see ourselves as God's Spirit and not our flesh.

This is the death we all must make. This is the baptism into the Spirit we all must take. This is the reason why even being the Spirit of God, Jesus allowed John to baptize Him to Himself. We all must take on Our Father's Spirit. We then must accept everything that comes with it.

We can no longer allow the things of the physical to influence the Spiritual. We must allow the Spirit to control the things in the physical world. It is the sum of our beliefs and actions that paints our reality. It is up to those who stand in agreement to bring Our Father's Kingdom into the physical. Jesus said, the kingdom of heaven is at hand. It is up to those who believe in Him to unite in His will. We cannot allow anything other than the love of Our Father to be our bond and glue. Our Father requires us all to love one another as He loved Jesus and as Jesus loved us...unconditionally, loving at all times and possessing charity. Then and only then will our joy be complete, and Our Father's house will be revealed for all to see. We must all abandon looking at ourselves as human beings and look at ourselves as the little pieces of Him we all are.

It is only in the Spirit, no excuse can be made. All are strengthened. All are knowledgeable. All have the same connection to God, the Father. Jesus dying paid the price for everyone to enter into heaven. We have to release the old in order to step into the new. We have to get rid of the part and accept the whole. The whole is Our Father's report and record on how to live life, not man's.

Romans 8:

> **38)** For I am persuaded, that neither death, nor life, nor angels, nor principalities, nor powers, nor things present, nor things to come, **39)** Nor height, nor depth,

nor any other creature, shall be able to separate us from the love of God, which is in Christ Jesus our Lord.

Hebrews 8:

10) For this is the covenant that I will make with the house of Israel after those days, saith the Lord; I will put my laws into their mind, and write them in their hearts: and I will be to them a God, and they shall be to me a people: **11)** And they shall not teach every man his neighbour, and every man his brother, saying, Know the Lord: for all shall know me, from the least to the greatest. **12)** For I will be merciful to their unrighteousness, and their sins and their iniquities will I remember no more. **13)** In that he saith, A new covenant, he hath made the first old. Now that which decayeth and waxeth old is ready to vanish away.

DAY
THREE
WALKING WITH GOD

The White Robe

Accept me as your guide.

Now that I have outlined the fact, the creation must come from the Creator. We understand we are all an extension of Our Father; we are all from the same source. I will turn the matter over to Our Father's Spirit, the Holy Ghost. If everything I know to be the truth is true, then the same message He has for me applies to us all. I pray, by this point, we have all decided to accept the truth of the Holy Spirit. The voice inside us is *not* of us. It never tells us what we want to hear. It always tells us what we need to hear.

It is our guide, and the very voice we are to harken to. I pray we all accept this voice as Our Father's way of talking to us via His Spirit, the Holy Ghost. Whatever Our Father has to give us will come next. I will no longer capitalize all the words God has placed inside me. Everything from this point on is our inner voice; it is the Holy Spirit in me talking to the Holy Spirit in you. It is the White Robe that is being offered to us all. The gift and an offering. Are you willing to put it on?

I am the Creator!

Stop giving credit to My creations, when you know something had to be the start of all creation. I am the Creator! With My words, I spoke everything into existence. I extended Myself to create all that is created. It is My life force that brings dust to life. It is My energy that allows for your life to exist. I am in the trees, as well as in the animals. I alone am the One who governs life. My energy goes inside of matter and brings into being all of life's creations.

I am depicted as male, because it takes My energy to go inside of the Earth to bring forth life. The matter used to create life is your mother. It takes both energy and matter for life to exist. Everything is of Me and in Me. Even what some consider evil is still of Me. I allow you to see the error in your ways, so you all can repent and return to Me. You were told to honor your mother and your father. To honor Me, you must honor the energy which is of Me for you to exist. Therefore, you ought to devote your energy to good, and to all things that will make you better. To honor your mother, you must take care of the Earth. I placed you in a garden and instructed you to tend the field. Stop abusing and polluting your mother.

Look inside.

Look inside yourself and see yourself for all you are. This is not meant to make you feel bad, but for you to identify yourself to yourself . I still love you, so smile. I never abandoned you; you abandoned Me. I already knew you would do all you have done. I had to let you grow into the understanding of Me. No one is truly ready to understand, I am inside of them. It can be a very scary or fearful thing to realize at first. I love you. The fear you should have of Me is the same as the reverence and respect you ought to have. The fear of going against Me should be rooted in life experiences. Every time you didn't follow after Me, you soon suffered in some way. So, laugh, smile, and be happy! I am here so your joy may be complete, not to scold you.

Relax.

I don't know who told you I was so uptight. Don't I bring laughter and joy to your mind all the time? Am I not the one telling you it is okay when you are feeling down? Is it not I who enters into your mind to instruct you when someone's opinion isn't valid? I came to add joy to your life. It is impossible to give you joy and not happiness. Joy is the source of happiness. Stop allowing man's thinking to trump Mine. Man will have you chasing after high points, but those same high points in life only reveal the lows you are trying to replace in your day-to-day life. Only through Me can you count it all joy.

I am always present.

You, yourselves, are always subject to the devil, hence the reason you may feel like I come and go. It is really the opposite. You come and you go in times of need. As Your Father, I will always be here to catch and guide you. The only thing you must ever do is ask for My advice, and I will answer all your prayers. No, not your worldly prayers for a Bugatti. I am speaking of spiritual prayers, like when you ask Me for peace, courage, endurance, strength, so forth, and so on.

Receive my love.

Every time you have asked for things of the Spirit, have I not given them to you? It isn't My fault, each time you have handed what I've given you, right back to Me. You asked for strength, I gave it to you. You asked for encouragement, you asked for perseverance, you asked for more patience, you asked all these things of Me, and I have given them freely to you. Learn to accept and keep all the things you ask of Me. It is the job of the devil to convince you to do otherwise.

Don't stress or become distracted.

Stop allowing man to place stress on you that I haven't placed on you. You are linked to the devil. You will forever be tainted, because you are a human being. You cannot do My will; only I can do My will. You must get out of My way, so you can be the vessel I always have intended you to be. You serve no purpose in My army, if you allow yourself to be distracted from the purpose for which I put you here. Love others and let your light shine freely. It is only your thoughts and objections that cause feelings and emotions to rise up.

Don't give in to materialism and marketing.

Entertainment and distractions are at an all-time high. Don't allow yourself to be given over to materialism and marketing. You must be in the world, but not of it. As long as you choose to be you, you can never choose to be Me. You are My opposition and main foe. Once you learn to overcome and conquer yourself, you will have the roadmap to helping others overcome themselves. This is the gospel and the good news.

Defeat the enemy.

Your sin is what perpetuates evil around the world. I have already defeated the devil. You can no longer use the excuse that what you do, or what happens is because of evil forces at work. To say that you suffer because of evil forces at work is to call Me a liar. I have already called you more than an overcomer and conqueror. Once you and your peers understand the schemes of the devil, it is up to all of you to be above them. The devil comes to pull at your emotions and feelings, to distract you from your main goal, and to cloud your judgment . Once you are in your own feelings, you begin to doubt yourself and everything you and I have worked for.

You alone are the antichrist.

You are all the antichrist. Any thinking that is not of Me is anti- (the exact opposite/reciprocal) what I am and what I stand for. Therefore, the antichrist must exist before the Holy Spirit comes and makes it Christlike. You all possess the ability to be legion; the worst thing any of you can do is try to clean out your temples and vessels on your own. Only I can cast out demons with My Spirit.

When you become clean on your own accord, the demon or demons you just kicked out, comes back with seven demons each who are even stronger than it or they were. If you keep cleansing yourself, you can easily see how you can end up with the entire demon legion. All the while thinking, you are striving for positivity. You will grow more negative than when you first started, if you do not allow Me, Your Father, full access and control. The temptations of life are always present. It is up to you to become tempted and give in. Just because they are there, it does not mean you go towards them.

In the prayer I gave you, it says, "lead us not to temptation". Just because it is there, it shouldn't matter. You must make yourself become above any impulse temptations can trigger. You must become the example I set before you to follow. It is not something to strive for. Stop saying, "Only Jesus can," and start saying, "We can." How can My Son reveal all My ways to you, but you still remain blind? You want to be blind, so you can remain in your current state and not evolve into what I have for you. I have told you, "Be ye perfect as Your Father in heaven is perfect." You have allowed man to come in and taint My very words and My very existence inside of you.

Allow me to enter.

You are My temple. You are to house Me, not control Me by thinking for Me. Never become clogged with the lusts of man's eyes. Little to none of My energy gets to flow through you. You blame Me for not giving you things I am trying to save you from. You are allowing another man to control you by chasing after fool's gold. When will you accept that I am the head of even you? No man is the head. The only way to fulfill My will is to accept your role and become an empty vessel. Any of your thoughts automatically taint My Spirit. Any of your actions set our actions off course. Just because I can use for good what the devil meant for bad, doesn't mean it is the way to learn. I have told you, all things are lawful, but all things are not expedient. All things are lawful, but all things do not edify. If you want to live a life edifying Me, and on your most expedient route and time frame, you must submit completely to My will.

Without charity, you are nothing.

Charity is my essence. It is everything I represent. How then, being a child of Mine, have you strayed so far from My teachings? You know right from wrong. However, you chose to think that getting over on your fellow man is good in My eyes. How wrong you are to ever think of yourself as smarter than I. I know your thoughts, before you can even begin to think. I give you the roadmap and access to things you can't access on your own. I allow you to roam in your mind and in the memories of your existence. I allow you to learn firsthand, in order for you to see, you cannot do what I do. Let alone, try to master it as I.

You are inferior to Me. You are an extension that has access to the whole; you are not the whole. Stop trying to make yourself greater than Me. Understand the olive branch I am offering, by allowing you to become My equal. Is it not I trying to teach you all of My ways? Many have learned and have been taught in error. I don't want to be your God. I am Your Father. One can be denied; the other cannot be refuted. I created you.

I love you!

My love for you as My child, allows Me to allow you to grow. Every child has a day when he or she must account for his or her maturity. At a certain age, you expect a child to be able to wake up and make his or her own cereal. Down the road, you expect a child to know how to use the microwave to cook a microwavable breakfast. Eventually, they can make their own breakfast. A child's lack of experience and size are the only things preventing them from performing certain tasks. They will be able to perform the tasks they cannot perform in the present moment, in the future.

You, My child, are the same. I already know. Due to your lack of maturity and understanding of My Spirit, you will err in the growing acknowledgment of who you are. However, My child, you are on the path to grow into what you are to become. Until you admit, you are growing inside of Me with every acknowledgment you make of Me. You can never grow as quickly as I would want you to grow. It is an instant, My child, not a lifetime. Once you fully accept Me, operating inside of Me is the only thing left to do.

I chose you.

I have already chosen you. You cannot choose Me. I am the potter, and I create as I so choose. I had to create a way for you all to be saved. My child by adoption is loved the same as My natural born. My natural- born cannot receive My love more than My adopted. Likewise, just because you are adopted, I give you no special treatment. The special treatment I offer is being My child. All of your ways will be revealed to you. You can continue to be a child, or you can choose to grow in Me. You must lay down your own thinking, knowledge, wisdom, and understanding before Me. You must choose to become a baby once again. I cannot teach an adult who's full of their own thinking. I can only teach those willing to be as a baby unto Me. Only then are you washed clean of your own thinking. You are all My children, whether you know yourself to be or not.

Let go of your pride, ego, and vanity.

Stop with all the catchphrases you have invented to represent Me in error. I command you all to love. I told you nothing of division. It is all of those who came before you, tainted with pride, vanity, and ego, who created this erroneous (sinful) thinking. Those are the ones who led you in error; those are the ones you continue to follow. The very things I have warned you against are the very things you do. I told you to trust no man. You have adapted your thinking to trust man before you even think of Me. Once everything is in total despair, you finally reach out to Me. I can recall all the times you reached out to Me in anger, for all the decisions I tried to prevent you from making. You are responsible for making the path twisted and winding, as opposed to straight.

I allowed the antichrist to exist, so all can learn of Me.

Don't fret, My child. Understand, I am here, and I always will be.

The antichrist is:

- All the teachings of man that are not Mine.
- All the self-proclaimed prophets, pastors, evangelists, and priests who are robbing My children blind.
- Everyone who is choosing to exploit My children, as opposed to lifting them up.
- Anyone willing to elevate themselves over another.
- Human nature.

- The system that has been teaching you anything other than you is an extension of Me.

All of you on Earth are brothers and sisters needing to unite in order to have a meaningful and peaceful existence.

I am responsible for all that is invented.

Stop thinking of just the Garden of Eden. Stop thinking technology isn't Mine. Understand, due to your being cut off from Me at an early age, because of your transgression, you have very limited knowledge of what I intend for you. I told you, I would allow the sinners to build up a world for My children to inherit. My Word will always be fulfilled. As some chase vain achievements and others' inventions, the truth remains: Everything that exists is because I have allowed it to become. All the technology that exists is Mine. I have given the answers for these things to be revealed. I am not here to make you subservient; I am here to make you My equal. All fathers want the best for their children. Why, then, do you continually doubt Me?

Jesus's flesh means nothing without My Spirit.

Many of you who take on My Spirit are supposed to be greater than even Jesus. You doubt who you are because you glorify Him as a man, not as the same Spirit you have inside of you because of My grace and mercy. No sibling submits to another. Even if your sibling has the best handwriting ever, you will compete with them to see who writes faster. Jesus isn't meant to be glorified in the sense of His physicality. He is to be glorified for releasing My Spirit. My glory is bestowed on Him by Him staying obedient to Me in the flesh. He is quoted saying not my will be done but Yours. Taking on His teachings is taking on His beliefs. If you believe like Him, then you must be My Child. Therefore, you are just like Him! Even greater acts can now be done because He is interceding on your behalf to Me.

There is only one Body of Christ.

A body divided can never stand. So many church buildings exist, but I have neither a church body nor kingdom at My disposal. I do not want what you value. I gave you what you valued, to show you the error in your ways. It wasn't meant for you to glorify them; it was meant for you to stop overvaluing them. Everyone wants to attain a brighter shine, but if you remove the lampshades of your own thoughts, pride, ego, and vanity, everyone would shine the same. For it is I who gives light, hence it is only I who can shine through you. Therefore, stop believing one is greater than the other. You are all the same. You all need to learn to have charity as the baseline of your thinking and actions. The path to charity may be extremely difficult, but it is your love and charity through which I said you should be known.

Stop allowing for division.

Stop separating yourselves because of flesh. Your flesh is where all the confusion lies. I have told you that you have to hate your father, mother, wife, children, brethren, sisters, and your own life also, in order to be My disciple. You must first become a disciple unto Me, with no outside influence. Only I should influence you. You should know who I am and what I stand for. The only way to study and show thyself approved is to trust Me. You should also know who I am not, and what I do not stand for. Allow your brothers and sisters in My Spirit to sharpen you. Someone in My name should state My name. If they are professing to be more than My servant, you should already know their message is tainted. I said, "call no man father or teacher, for I alone am the ruler of My kingdom." I only need vessels.

My Spirit is alive amongst you.

Accept the honor and privilege, it is to be considered a brother or sister in My Spirit. Humble yourself to accept there is no greater honor bestowed on anyone. I have already attempted to make you My equal for your entire life. You chose not to follow My every step. In the old days, when the people spoke of fearing Me. They feared going against the Word I spoke to them. Because the people living in that time were more obedient. I didn't have to communicate with them as often. My Spirit was alive and amongst them. It was when they questioned Me and My blessings, your forefathers allowed man to corrupt the Earth. This was first established by the appointment of kings and queens, followed by the establishment of governments and territories. Now, in the present day, it is big businesses and corporations.

Stop giving My attention away.

Samuel tried to warn you. I hope you now understand. It was I who, through him, tried to warn you. I cannot rob you of your curiosities. If I robbed you of your curiosities. You will say that I am a dictating God, not a loving Father. You will sin against Me all the more. I gave you the law as a tool to show you what I wanted for you. You looked at it as, I was telling you what you had to do, as opposed to your obedience saving you from your wicked and evil ways. Most importantly, my will saves you from falling victim to another's erroneous thinking and evil ways. I gave you a way to never be controlled by another man. I have always told you, I am jealous. I am not jealous in an unloving sense. I am jealous of the attention you give your fellow man, because I so desperately am trying to get your attention. I, Myself, am begging and pleading from the inside of you, yet you still reject pieces and parts of Me. You then blame your lack of obedience on another. Constantly murmuring and complaining to Me, what another has done to you. Instead of abiding in the example of love, I have set forth for you.

Return My prodigal child.

When will you trust My word? You know right from wrong. You know I have made it clear to not offend your brothers and sisters. Who are you to limit what I have told you? Isn't the wayward son still my son? Therefore, understand you are all my prodigal children. I am waiting with open arms to receive all of you. Likewise, if you already have come to know Me and have basked in My presence. Who are you to rob your brothers and sisters of the same love, I showed you upon your return? Stop acting like a spoiled child, who feels, the love given to another child robs them of the love I have for them. I am love. Just as I have prepared a feast for you. I have prepared a feast for them. Haven't I said, I would set a feast before you? What you decide to eat is up to you. I have given you an endless amount of good fruit. I know it must be put into you, for it to come out of you. Stop eating the poison fruit of your own thoughts. They all stem from the lust of your eye and the pride of life.

Give control to Me.

The fruit of the enemy is the lust of the eye. The lust of the eye will always draw you away from Me and have you tempted. When will you realize, the flesh cannot offer you a fraction of what I can? The flesh compels you to splurge and spend, but you never attain anything. I am trying to compel you to save and invest in your true freedom. I give you the keys to attain more life. I told you to tend the fields and be good stewards of the animals. You have abandoned both, in your attempt to live out a worldly dream. When will you accept, all the dreams you imagine for yourself are limited from the beginning? You don't know everything I know, therefore you can't think of the things I want to give and bestow upon you. Your true freedom is what you blindly pursue. Independence is the only freedom that is real.

I require love in the form of charity.

The lust of the eye is surpassed, when you choose to listen to Me. I never wanted it to be deemed commandments. I wanted you to understand Me from the beginning. I allowed My Son to be an example of how to live life. He served others. He forgave when others didn't. He taught those whom others would not teach. He did not look down on others. He did not chase after worldly riches. He did not claim to be better or try to outperform others.

Stop giving yourself over to your own thinking and lustful eye. The attempts to create something better than Me are foolish. Get rid of all the false pathways of life. The entire purpose of life is to attain and understand unconditional love. If everything points to love, why keep talking about love? My children, at what point do you listen and perform the duty of Charity? Inside of love, there is no hate. I have told you over and over, I want you with a pure heart. How then do you come to Me as the Creator and question My task unto you?

Stop favoring man's system.

Start applying common sense. You do not have to recreate the wheel. I have laid all the resources in front of you. Stop using things that take years and years to manifest, serve the purpose of something that can be grown in a year. Furthermore, stop eating seedless fruit. I have commanded you to grow seed-bearing fruit. The lack of seeds is the lack of future substance for life. Stop allowing a system invented by man to enslave Me. Therefore, be the best version of you and stop allowing man to eclipse the reasoning I have given you. This is displayed to you in multiple ways. They demonstrate you must follow them over Me. Who is this pope? Why do you blindly follow the blind? No man is better than the other. It is My Spirit inside of an individual that separates one from another. Am I not inside all of you? Am I not the God of all flesh? Likewise, I have told you: One man esteemeth one day above another: another esteemeth every day alike. Let every man be fully persuaded in his own mind. Romans 5:14 (KJV). Stop allowing your fellow man to trump Me. Even those who still esteem one day above the other. You have allowed man to change My sabbath day. Is not Saturday the true seventh day? I would hope you now understand, I am here with you every day!

Return to Me.

Therefore, every second of every moment of every day, My child, I want you to allow Me to be there for you. Protecting and shielding you, from the constant bombardment of stress you are under. Stop allowing others to divide you. Your own doubts are what limit Me in your life. You constantly know the right thing to do. The little wiggle room you give yourself to remain outside of My complete will is the biggest problem. You look at all the good in order to excuse the little bad, but realize, the little wiggle room you give yourself is the reason My Body does not connect. Only unconditional love can be the glue to connect all the many members of My Body. Therefore, stop limiting My Body with your judgements.

Wear your appropriate armor .

The second you judge; you open yourself up to division. Stop judging. If you judge by My standards, you cannot judge. Your Savior always corrected and forgave. Although, someone on the outside can look at this as Him having to first judge in order to correct. I will inform you. You all know right from wrong, therefore to recognize wrong isn't judging. You knowing right from wrong is having discernment. Stop robbing yourself of the ability to develop a high level of discernment, by looking at it as judgment . Your judgment is how you process your life and memories. All the thoughts and thinking you carry along with you as your own defense system. These thoughts protect what you feel and view as right and wrong. In other words, it is your set of rules, not Mine. However, I have already told you the proper armor and attire to wear in life. You fail to accept My instructions are out of love and assistance, not control and dictatorship.

If you become obedient to Me, no man will be able to corrupt your mind, because they can't corrupt Me. By you believing and becoming My child. You now have My Spirit, and My Spirit cannot be tainted.

Your freedom is in charity.

Love is an action. Charity is applying it to everyone. Therefore, the action of love builds up one another. Charity is building up everyone you meet. If you choose to support your fellow man, no one will have to take care of your fellow man. By all of you knowing the truth, there is no way to swindle the masses. The truth frees you from chasing after money. Do you envision needing money in Heaven? Money is a tool used to enslave.

Do not think all have escaped slavery. The presentation of it has just changed. I intended for you to be free to yourself and to live out your own existence. You should be effecting change, in whatever way I guide you, to be an asset to your fellow man. Loving one another automatically covers each of you an estimated 7.6 billion times over. Therefore, you are automatically more covered via love, than whatever other covering you can give yourself times 7.6 billion. The only thing preventing My love from flowing is each of My Children being individuals and not united. Until you accept the simple truth, the propaganda in the form of news and media will continue to have you all divided from each other. It is easy to come up with statistics and information to deter you from coming together. All can agree working together lightens the overall load. Why does the thought of another's load being lightened more, or someone getting over, make you not choose to still lighten your load?

Never take off your armor !

These are the traps to which you open yourself when you decide to think and not follow after My teachings and instructions. My teachings and instructions will not allow the devil to tempt you, therefore no man-made system can entrap you either. When you identify the devil to the meaning of a man's thinking outside of My will. You can realize the purpose for My armor and who and what you are up against.

Ephesians 6:

> **10)** Finally, my brethren, be strong in the Lord, and in the power of his might. **11)** Put on the whole armor of God, that ye may be able to stand against the wiles of the devil. **12)** For we wrestle not against flesh and blood, but against principalities, against powers, against the rulers of the darkness of this world, against spiritual wickedness in high places. **13)** Wherefore take unto you the whole armor of God, that ye may be able to withstand in the evil day, and having done all, to stand. **14)** Stand therefore, having your loins girt about with truth, and having on the breastplate of righteousness; **15)** And your feet shod with the preparation of the gospel of peace; **16)** Above all, taking the shield of faith, wherewith ye shall be able to quench all the fiery darts of the wicked. **17)** And take the helmet of salvation, and the sword of the Spirit, which is the word of God: **18)** Praying always with all prayer and supplication in the Spirit, and watching thereunto with all perseverance and supplication for all saints;

Allow me to lead.

You have allowed yourself to fall victim to the schemes of those same people you are at war against. If I am not inside your leaders, how can you expect any form of justice? You must reach the conclusion, you can't. To pray for your leaders only makes sense if they are under My stewardship. If they are carnal, I have told you; they are still enmity against Me. Therefore, I have no control over them. In all the democratic systems in existence throughout the world, stop thinking it takes a special person or bloodline to lead. It takes a servant humbly submitting to My will to lead.

You will be able to identify them because you can now identify the good within you. Instead of trusting yourself, who can easily be tricked and deceived by the enemy, trust Me. You always feel when evil is present. It isn't something you need to identify; it is something you need to accept. You don't have to learn how to feel the negative aura of another. It is something you all can feel and naturally identify. Until you learn to transform the evil around you, part ways from it. Once you understand, you are light and positivity. You will attract darkness and negativity. Bestow the love (light and positivity) onto the hateful (dark and evil) individual. However, do not go blindly through the world throwing your pearls before swine.

Be like-minded in love.

A swine is a person fully engulfed in the carnal mind, someone who wants nothing to do with the Spiritual side of life. All the time and energy you invest in swine will be trampled and stomped upon. Furthermore, he or she will rend you; "to rend" means to violently tear you into two or more pieces, and to cause great emotional pain to a person's heart. When you understand these principles, the only person fit to deal with swine is someone prepared to cast out demons. A demon is any negative spirit that is affecting someone else. Demons most often come in the form of memories, thinking, and mindsets. A memory starts to make you think, which changes your mindset and triggers emotions; the devil then latches onto those emotions. The negative emotion caused by your thinking is how the devil enters your mind, therefore your spirit. You must accept, every time you are negative, you are allowing the devil to piggyback off you, and to exist because of your existence.

Realize, My Child, that there is nothing more important than what I, Myself, have to teach and instruct you. Stop allowing the critics of man to eclipse the relationship I have established with you. Stop allowing your own pride to rob you of the growth I have put in your path. Everyone I have put into your path is a piece of the puzzle for you to learn. You must open your mind to the possibility of everyone being covered. I have explained, time and time again, this is My Will. If you are to bear your own cross and take up My charge, I expect you to elevate My people to your newfound understanding. Have I not done it for you? Stop treating others with anything short of the love I have given unto you. Stop thinking the road you took to attain love is more valuable than another's. What matters is what you do, once you attain the proper knowledge of love.

Love one another.

Stop allowing people to profess childish ways so bold and loudly. They are only adding to the confusion. You add to it as well, by spreading the half-truths I am trying to get rid of. The totality of it all is loving one another. All the bickering of who, what, why, and how takes away from the performing and doing. I said to do My Will, and everything will be added. If you know what I have for you is better than what you can imagine, why are you scared of performing My Will? My people have killed Me every time I have come to save them. If they did not kill Me off, they tried to greatly minimize My teachings. If the application of My Word is misinterpreted by My people, what purpose does My Word serve?

Abandon carnality and the world's ways.

Stop allowing My Word to be stripped from history. Throughout history, the Church and the governments and ruling entities have been at war with each other. I have given you the cornerstone to build on. Nothing can be fulfilled without you first repenting of your carnal mind. Once you strip yourself of your carnality, you can see to whom I have given the cornerstone to build with. Nothing can be fulfilled without you first repenting of your carnal mind. Once you strip yourself of your carnality, you can see you are an extension of My Spirit. Do not fall into the trap of wanting to be your own spirit. You were your own spirit while you were in the flesh. Do not have to relearn all the teachings I have already given you to get to this point. Your fleshly experience exposed your free will. It showed you how you thought, and all the problems that will continue to arise, based upon your own thinking. You cannot bring your thinking into Me. You are enmity against Me. You are My main opposition and foe. You are the one constantly getting in My way. To connect with the rest of My body, you must be willing to part.

Accept love is the only way.

Love is the glue that must be present, to attach and connect with another. Love is the glue uniting and building everyone back up to their intended purpose. Love and the spreading of love are the foundation for My kingdom. The unity of the entire Body is My will. The differences and prejudices you have developed have nothing to do with Me. I commanded you to love. In love there is no room for you to harbor hate. Therefore, whatever hate you still have in your mind, you must accept that it is of you and your carnal father, the devil. Only an individual of the carnal mind can still be operating in a sinful state. The devil is the father of carnality. Escape the devil and hell by learning to love as I love.

Until you accept My love, you will never receive My cooling waters. Understand, My Spirit is what you thirst after. Once you receive My Spirit, you shall thirst no more. You will then be able to put out your own fires. Therefore, hell is no longer a place for your soul. You will stop tormenting yourself according to the perceptions man has placed on you. You will automatically gain the peace that passes all understanding. Once, you are exposed to all the fires, you have created on your own. You can start the process of putting out fires and adding life to your existence. Until you apply My cooling waters, you will constantly set ablaze all the instructions I am trying to give you. Therefore, you must accept My teachings in order for you to grow in love.

Your purpose is to perform My will.

You all have the same purpose: To escape the traps laid forth by man and to step into the Spiritual side of yourself. Once inside the Holy Spirit, therefore Me, you will be able to see everyone brings and offers something. Stop discrediting what another brings or offers to the Body. He or she will grow in the Holy Spirit, just as everyone has grown before them. It is not until you stop looking for the benefits a person has to offer, can you see and realize what he or she offers Me. A simple smile can be the best thing that encourages another person that day. A simple, "How are you doing? I love you. God bless. Good morning, afternoon or evening," allows another to know that he or she is cared for and thought of. This is the very same confirmation you look for.

I have told you that you are blessed to be a blessing. I didn't exploit your ignorance. I elevated you out of it. If you are to perform My will, you must learn to give knowledge and understanding to others. Do not exploit others because of their lack of it. Being a stumbling block to your fellow man is deeper than some frivolous sin. If you enslave someone for their entire life, whose fault is it if he or she amounts to less than what I intended for him or her? Is it the person's fault for not doing better, or is it your fault for not elevating him or her to the level you know they should attain or have?

Repent and become My friend.

I will never keep someone as My servant. Who are you to keep someone as yours? If I have elevated My servants to My friends, who are you to enslave My friends? Are you greater than I am? If you truly treated someone as you treat yourself, you would automatically understand that you don't want to be someone's servant. Therefore, do not perform things outside of My Will and claim to be inside My Will, which is for everyone to understand, they are My Sons and Daughters. Therefore, as My Children, no man is above them.

You are one body with many members. Until you unite with others, it is impossible for you to perform My Will, and acknowledge it includes more than just you. You have called out to Me in anger and frustration, acting as though I have left or abandoned you. I have already said, I will neither leave you nor forsake you. You have abandoned Me. You have abandoned Me by abandoning love. You are mad at Me because you and others are not performing My love in its proper form. You all have allowed man to be left unchecked. I told you to rebuke thy brother when he sins against you. You have chosen to spare his/her feelings, instead of telling the truth. Then the trap of not rebuking him or her plays out its course in your mind and life. You become resentful and bitter at yourself, not Me. I told you what to do. It was you who did not follow Me and rebuke him or her.

Man cannot give you My reward.

Love works! However, the current application of love does not work! You have allowed love to become tainted by things that are not of love. Instead of taking the time to perfect love, you have allowed yourself to become defeated by the response of man when you give love. Whose reward are you seeking, men or Mine? If it is Mine, then man's reaction to the instructions I give you doesn't matter. If you are seeking man's reward, then you aren't a child of Mine. Stop trying to find a reason why love doesn't work and acknowledge the results when you apply My instruction of love to life. You will find that My yoke is easy, and My burdens are light. The world has taught you all the things that hold you back from giving yourself over to Me.

Charity has always been the answer.

Stop dividing My Body because of your own thoughts, ego, and opinions. Your own thoughts are the reason My Body cannot stand. I have given proper instructions to follow. I have commanded you to apply grace and mercy on your fellow brothers and sisters. Anything short of unconditional and unlimited love is not of Me. Therefore, to view yourself as Mine, you must be a representation of Me. Love is the answer you all are so desperately searching for. The kingdom must be built on charity.

Charity allows everyone to be a part of the Body. I have already told you not to get caught up in the divisiveness of the world. I have told you that love works, and love is access into My kingdom. I have left a written account for you to understand the great multitude which no man could number, of all nations, and kindreds, and people, and tongues, standing before the throne, and before the Lamb, clothed with white robes, and with palm branches in their hands. Those clothed in white robes are all of you who choose to accept My Spirit and wear the robe that comes with it.

I am the God of Life

I am the God of the living. Stop stressing over death. You are life. Stop identifying yourself as a mortal. The only way to view yourself as a mortal is to abandon the fact that you are an extension of My Spirit, therefore My energy. I separated the water from the heavens, then separated the waters inside of Heaven to create dry land. Therefore, if I started with heaven, how can you be outside of Heaven? You can't! You act as though My physical presence should change My existence. I have told you unless you love your brother who is seen, you can't love Me who is unseen. I am your brother. He is I and I am you. You are all Me. Why would I impoverish and abuse Myself?

You are all trying to make it to heaven. Many have confused what it means to make it into Heaven. The race is not to the swift, nor the battle to the strong, neither yet bread to the wise, nor yet riches to men of understanding, nor yet favor to men of skill; time and chance happeneth to them all. The same time and chances are given to you all. Just because you acquire a certain attribute does not mean you will receive the reward because of the possession of a trait. It is only when you put that skill or trait to use that you will see the benefits from it.

You are already inside of Heaven.

If you are already in Heaven, how can you get to Heaven? Is not the atmosphere I give you Heaven? Does not the life I afford you, allow you into My courts? When will you accept, it is My Will *not* being carried out that makes up the mental torture all of you are in? As for leaving Earth, the task I gave you was to take care of Earth. Why are you so quick to give up My instructions for death? If I am the God of the living, I bring the dead to life. I am energy, the Maker and Giver of all. The account you give, or will give, you are already giving. Take the time to repent from your ways while I give you the opportunity.

Stop striving to reach outer space. The same beings from outer space want to reach you. Stop thinking, something on the opposite side of the universe is better than what I have created for you. I called and deemed everything good. Due to your vain pursuits, you have corrupted what I have called good, in your attempts to make something great in mankind's eyes. In the pursuit of greatness, you have created the opposite of it. Every time you, as an individual, strive for greatness, you rob another individual of being good. Why are you so vain? You pursue greatness, when I have given you good? When will you get to the conclusion, My good is your spectacular? You have become so separated from the truth. The ugly lie the world presents appears beautiful in your eyes. Everything is perspective-based. If your vantage point is tainted and corrupt, your perspective will be also. You must accept, you must return to what I have given you.

Release experiencing Heaven, by building My Kingdom.

You all have to work together to build Heaven, as I have instructed you. You have all the tools and resources at your disposal. Stop wasting time learning about Me, when you already know Me. I am everything good. I am all the love and positivity in the world. I am good. This can seem to some, as I am vain and greedy, but I am love. I want you to be a part of Me. The current system is ineffective. With all the work being done in My Name, why isn't My will for you being fulfilled? The application of My Word has been performed in error. You have allowed My Church to become a building. My Church is you. My Church and Kingdom are one and the same. It is you and your brothers and sisters.

For My Church to rise, the currently flawed church concept must be torn down. You have built many church buildings, dividing My true Church. In some neighborhoods, I see many church buildings in the same area. My Spirit is the same. Why, once exposed to Me, do you feel as if I am not enough? Why do you think it is more than simply listening and obeying Me? I know you know My thoughts over your own. I know you can recall now, all the times I have tried to lead and guide you out of choices you have made. You must unite with your brothers and sisters; not gather with people you already know. You go and sit and hear stories of how I have helped others. You learn of the sufferings My people endured because of their disobedience towards Me. Why then do you think this current generation is any different?

Apply My teachings for independence and freedom.

Start applying My teachings! It serves no purpose to learn of Me and not apply My Will over your life. My Will in your life does not align with you simply learning of Me. I have stated, faith without works is dead. I have given you the blueprint for life. I have told you to tend the field first. Many of you have relegated tending the field as something beneath you. To tend the field, you must first possess a piece of land. Furthermore, I have told you, once you tend the field, then and only then do you build your house. Many of you have houses without a tended field. How can this be? You have gone against My teachings, and your own pride doesn't allow you to repent from your error.

You fail to see the value in what I have spoken to you. If you were to tend your own field, you would have your own food. I have told you to eat food only grown in My name. Instead, you act as if someone who mass produces food, grew that food in My honor and in My name or in My love. There is a reason your food is now lacking nutrients and proper edification to My temple. Furthermore, growing food is not only for the health of My temple but also for your true independence. When you have a meal waiting at all times, the need for you to be enslaved to another is lessened.

With all thy getting, get an understanding.

The first thing you must do before you apply My teachings, is understand My teachings. Before you get ahead of yourself, water must be present in order for you to tend the field. You have allowed man to control all the resources I have given to you. Few of My children are applying My teachings. By few applying My teachings, few of My children even realize the intrusions man's thinking has on My will.

If you were to tend the field and create your own food source, when you add shelter, there is nothing man can offer you less than your true worth. By rejecting My teachings, you have subjected yourself to man's control. You have allowed man to place limits and restrictions on resources. Time has become the only resource most have to offer. Most are underpaid and overworked because you fail to become independent of your own accord. To be independent is everyone's ultimate goal, whether they realize it or not. It is easier to achieve your independence with the help of others. The more and more you follow after Me; the more and more your true needs are met. The more and more you meet your true needs; the more surplus you will have.

Unless action is present, there is no life to your faith.

I have told you to invest in Me. In order to invest in Me, you must invest in life. Stop being persuaded to invest in man's system. Man's system is meant to stay in control. The only way for man's system to stay in control is to keep you in submission. The way they keep you in submission is to limit your finances. You have all these great ideas for your fellow man. Without the money to carry out My Will, you can never perform any of those ideas. All the thinking any of you can do, and the faith you all build up, is nothing without action. My Word says faith *without works is dead.* No matter what you believe or stand for if your actions aren't performing the faith you believe, there is no life to your faith. Therefore, all your faith is dead, because you never breathed life into it via action. Life is bringing things into existence. If it doesn't exist, it is dead. You create the reality you want by performing the actions required to make it happen. You can believe in My Kingdom all you want. The actions it takes to bring it to existence are already written.

My Will being performed releases Heaven.

If you truly treated people how you wanted to be treated, you would see that no one wants to be a worker and a worker alone. You don't mind working. However, you do mind being exploited. Any man or woman being exploited suffers internally. The Body of Christ must stand. With the Body standing, offers to elevate My children would be the norm. Offers to teach others true independence would be the norm. People taking care of one another would be the norm. People would not try to use the knowledge I have allowed them to possess, to enslave My people. Heaven is where I reign supreme. My children, I dwell amongst you when you allow Me to. You must release Me. I am inside of you. If you put a lampshade on Me, I cannot shine. You feel my light on the inside. Allow Me to shine on the outside.

Your own judgment and criticisms of others are the reasons you dim My light. You have allowed man to convince you that the majority of you are evil. All of you are evil without My guidance. You are special, My Child, but you must understand that everyone is special. If everyone is special, stop allowing the fact you are special to make you feel superior to another. If you are all special, you are all equal. In My Spirit, no man can esteem himself over his brother. Therefore, if no man can esteem himself over his brother, how can you have servants? Stop allowing your pride, ego, and vanity to take the place of My will!

It is time to unite.

It is up to you all to gather in unison. I have given you My prayer, but few have taken the time to see. Everything I stated was plural. I stated "our," "we," and "us." Why then can't you see that you need to unite with your brothers and sisters in order to perform My Will? You have allowed false prophets and the antichrist to persuade you to do things different from My teachings. I have tried to give you My sword, and My sword is My Word. Few attempt to pick it up, let alone go on My attack. You must understand the full marching orders before you go on My attack.

What is overlooked is this: My Spirit must swing My sword. I told you, the sword of the Holy Spirit is My Word. Unless you have My Spirit, you do not know how to use My sword. You fail to grasp My sword is love. Hence in Revelation, I have informed you, *he that killeth with the sword, must be killed with the sword.* Only a carnally dead man can possess Me. Here is the patience and the faith of the saints.

Having patience unto life is love.

The patience we must possess is the Sword (Our Father's Love) will come back and slay those who have used it. None of My words are unto death, but unto life. I have come to give you life and life more abundantly. How then can you, My Child, use my Word unto death? It cannot be. My Child, I need you to see. The second someone acknowledges Me, even in error, My Spirit is upon them. Once My Spirit is upon them, they are subject to My control. They have allowed me to exist inside of their thoughts and thinking. No matter how negatively a person may present themselves, the truth of Me is now alive inside of them. My love is now a seed sprouting inside of them waiting to grow.

Collect the harvest as you plant and water seeds.

Inside of love, you must choose willingly and joyfully to labor in love. When you choose willingly to labor in love, you are a joy to be around. By being a joy to be around, you plant seeds of joy in every negative person you have been around. Your natural joy is what negative people are searching for. I am starting to grow in their lives. The more examples of Me they run across; the more light and water there will be for the seed inside them to grow. This is when you must allow My Spirit to work. You can't expect someone who is just getting to know Me to understand all of my ways. We all know, they know wrong from right. However, the reason to always choose right isn't clear to them yet.

The moment anyone admits I exist, they can never un-admit the thought of Me. Therefore, deep down in everyone's thinking, I exist. Some are more skeptical than others, hence the reason My light has to shine brightly amongst My children. The skeptics wouldn't be skeptics, if they saw more examples of pure light. No one can doubt Me, when they see Me in My children. The carnal mind is built and rooted in doubt and fear. The more fear and doubt a person has in their thinking, the more space the devil has and must operate in their thinking. The more the devil overtakes a person's thinking, the more love needs to be labored in. The same space the devil overtook is now overcome and reclaimed for my use.

Stop doubting My existence in others.

The more you acknowledge Me existing, the more you see that I exist. The more you see that I exist, the more you are willing to die to your carnality. Therefore, the patience required of My Children is the allowance of Me to work. In addition, for My Children to continue in My faith, swinging My Sword of Truth, by doing your part in unconditional and unlimited love. The more love there is on display, the less space the devil has to operate. You must be willing to see past what is being presented to you. Go out and interact with one another. You must willingly put on the white robe and accept there is only one way to wear it. The patience to allow love to work is love itself. As Your Father, I am looking for you to allow My love to work. There must be a starting point for My salvation being given to all. It starts with each one of you who claims to love Me, displaying it to everyone you meet.

The more peace and love being shown, the easier it is for Me to work. Allow your eyes to be opened. I have said,

Matthew 6:

> **22)** The light of the body is the eye: if therefore thine eye be single, thy whole body shall be full of light. **23)** But if thine eye be evil, thy whole body shall be full of darkness. If therefore the light that is in thee be darkness, how great is that darkness! **24)** No man can serve two masters: for either he will hate the one, and love the other; or else he will hold to the one, and despise the other. Ye cannot serve God and mammon."

Abandon your flesh and in part thinking.

Never look out from fleshly eyes. Always possess My Spiritual eye. The flesh will automatically darken My light. The flesh is the darkest entity out there. Your flesh is what links you to legion. When you stop being fooled by the lust of the carnal eye, you can see clearly. You can ask a class of kindergarteners, if they would rather be a slave or have to use the bathroom outside. All in the classroom would say, "go use the bathroom outside." They are not tainted by the world. However, do I even have to ask you? You have made your choice. You must repent from your own thinking.

1 Corinthians 13:

> **10)** But when that which is perfect is come, then that which is in part shall be done away. **11)** When I was a child, I spake as a child, I understood as a child, I thought as a child: but when I became a man, I put away childish things. **12)** For now we see through a glass, darkly; but then face to face: now I know in part; but then shall I know even as I am known. **13)** And now abideth faith, hope, charity, these three; but the greatest of these is charity.

The only way to become perfect is to realize that you are operating in part. These are the revelations your forefathers rejected.

Matthew 23:

> **37)** O Jerusalem, Jerusalem, thou that killest the prophets, and stonest them which are sent unto thee, how often would I have gathered thy children together, even as a hen gathereth her chickens under her wings, and ye would not! **38)** Behold, your house is left unto you desolate. **39)** For I say unto you, Ye shall not see me henceforth, till ye shall say, Blessed is he that cometh in the name of the Lord.

Acceptance becomes obedience.

You must understand that the leaders of your church back then didn't accept My teachings. So why now do you allow the same to persist? How hard is it to accept that I have commanded you to love? This is the very commandment you still reject. You reject it because of human nature. You reject it because of man's doings. How do you think I feel, My child? This is why Samuel prayed. He understood My pain due to you choosing your fellow man over Me.

Hebrews 5:

1) For every high priest taken from among men is ordained for men in things pertaining to God, that he may offer both gifts and sacrifices for sins: **2)** Who can have compassion on the ignorant, and on them that are out of the way; for that he himself also is compassed with infirmity. **3)** And by reason hereof he ought, as for the people, so also for himself, to offer for sins. **4)** And no man taketh this honour unto himself, but he that is called of God, as was Aaron. **5)** So also Christ glorified not himself to be made an high priest; but he that said unto him, Thou art my Son, today have I begotten thee. **6)** As he saith also in another place, Thou art a priest for ever after the order of Melchisedec. **7)** Who in the days of his flesh, when he had offered up prayers and supplications with strong crying and tears unto him that was able to save him from death, and was heard in that he feared; **8)** Though he were a Son, yet learned he obedience by the things which he suffered; **9)**And being made perfect, he became the author of eternal salvation unto all them that obey him; **10)** Called of God an high priest after the order of Melchisedec.

I am the Creator and transformer.

Stop being misled! I Myself transformed Jesus! I begot Him on the day I chose Him as My vessel. He learned of Me the same as you are learning of Me. I knew He would grow into Me. However, life had to allow Him to mature for Me to dwell freely inside of Him. He learned obedience by the things He suffered.

James 1:

> **2)** My brethren, count it all joy when ye fall into divers temptations; **3)** Knowing this, that the trying of your faith worketh patience. **4)** But let patience have her perfect work, that ye may be perfect and entire, wanting nothing. **5)** If any of you lack wisdom, let him ask of God, that giveth to all men liberally, and upbraideth not; and it shall be given him. **6)** But let him ask in faith, nothing wavering. For he that wavereth is like a wave of the sea driven with the wind and tossed. **7)** For let not that man think that he shall receive any thing of the Lord. **8)** A double- minded man is unstable in all his ways.

I am showing you your thoughts and thinking, so yours can become like Mine. Do not lose your heart. Until you accept, you are My Child. You will never accept the love in My teachings. You will always view Me as a dictating God, as opposed to a loving Father.

Hebrews 12:

> **5)** And ye have forgotten the exhortation which speaketh unto you as unto children, My son, despise not thou the chastening of the Lord, nor faint when thou art rebuked of him: **6)** For whom the Lord loveth he chasteneth, and scourgeth every son whom he receiveth. **7)** If ye endure chastening, God dealeth with you as with sons; for what son is he whom the father chasteneth not? **8)** But if ye be without chastisement, whereof all are partakers, then are ye bastards, and not sons. **9)** Furthermore we have had fathers of our flesh which corrected us, and we gave them reverence: shall we not much rather be in subjection unto the Father of spirits, and live? **10)** For they verily for a few days

chastened us after their own pleasure; but he for our profit, that we might be partakers of his holiness. **11)** Now no chastening for the present seemeth to be joyous, but grievous: nevertheless afterward it yieldeth the peaceable fruit of righteousness unto them which are exercised thereby. **12)** Wherefore lift up the hands which hang down, and the feeble knees; **13)** And make straight paths for your feet, lest that which is lame be turned out of the way; but let it rather be healed. **14)** Follow peace with all men, and holiness, without which no man shall see the Lord. Take up your cross.

Bear your cross and self-evaluate.

Take responsibility for your actions. It is My will that you learn of Me. You will learn of Me by learning of yourself. The only way to wash and clean you against Me is to first understand My Spirit.

Galatians 5:

22) But the fruit of the Spirit is love, joy, peace, long-suffering, gentleness, goodness, faith, **23)** Meekness, temperance: against such there is no law. **24)** And they that are Christ's have crucified the flesh with the affections and lusts. **25)** If we live in the Spirit, let us also walk in the Spirit. **26)** Let us not be desirous of vain glory, provoking one another, envying one another.

Operate from My Spirit.

Humble yourself to understand it is you who removes yourself from My presence, by not being obedient to My Spirit. If you are inside of My Spirit, you are inside of the law. My Spirit breaks not the law. The law is different from man's traditions. Do not think that with the progression of time, the prophets I have sent you were incorrect. By not taking My teachings along the way, you have strayed completely against My teachings.

Before you bring up the Old Testament to Me, I hope you understand the ignorance of your questioning Me. However, I know the minds of My Children. Until you can accept, I am all-knowing, and you aren't. How can I reveal My truths to you without you first accepting My Spirit?

John 15:

> **13)** Greater love hath no man than this, that a man lay down his life for his friends. **14)** Ye are my friends, if ye do whatsoever I command you. **15)** Henceforth I call you not servants; for the servant knoweth not what his lord doeth: but I have called you friends; for all things that I have heard of my Father I have made known unto you. **16)** Ye have not chosen me, but I have chosen you, and ordained you, that ye should go and bring forth fruit, and that your fruit should remain: that whatsoever ye shall ask of the Father in my name, he may give it to you . **17)** These things I command you, that ye love one another. **18)** If the world hates you, you know that it hated me before it hated you. **19)** If ye were of the world, the world would love its own: but because ye are not of the world, but I have chosen you out of the world, therefore the world hateth you. **20)** Remember the word that I said unto you, The servant is not greater than his lord. If they have persecuted me, they will also persecute you; if they have kept my saying, they will keep yours also. **21)** But all these things will they do unto you for my name's sake, because they know not him that sent me. **22)** If I had not come and spoken unto them, they had not had sin: but now they have no cloak for their sin. **23)** He that hateth me hateth my Father also. **24)** If I had not done among them the works which none other man did, they had not had sin: but now have they both seen and hated both me and my Father. **25)** But this cometh to pass, that the word might be fulfilled that is written in their law, They hated me without a cause.

26) But when the Comforter is come, whom I will send unto you from the Father, even the Spirit of truth, which proceedeth from the Father, he shall testify of me: **27)** And ye also shall bear witness, because ye have been with me from the beginning. I can only lead those of me.

Lay down your own life, so you can be resurrected in Mine.

John 8:

43) Why do ye not understand my speech? even because ye cannot hear my word. **44)** Ye are of your father the devil, and the lusts of your father ye will do. He was a murderer from the beginning, and abode not in the truth, because there is no truth in him. When he speaketh a lie, he speaketh of his own: for he is a liar, and the father of it. **45)** And because I tell you the truth, ye believe me not. **46)** Which of you convinceth me of sin? And if I say the truth, why do ye not believe me? **47)** He that is of God heareth God's words: ye therefore hear them not, because ye are not of God. **48)** Then answered the Jews, and said unto him, Say we not well that thou art a Samaritan, and hast a devil? **49)** Jesus answered, I have not a devil; but I honour my Father, and ye do dishonour me. **50)** And I seek not mine own glory: there is one that seeketh and judgeth. **51)** Verily, verily, I say unto you, If a man keep my saying, he shall never see death. **52)** Then said the Jews unto him, Now we know that thou hast a devil. Abraham is dead, and the prophets; and thou sayest, If a man keep my saying, he shall never taste of death. **53)** Art thou greater than our father Abraham, which is dead? and the prophets are dead: whom makest thou thyself? **54)** Jesus answered, If I honour myself, my honour is nothing: it is my Father that honoureth me; of whom ye say, that he is your God: **55)** Yet ye

> have not known him; but I know him: and if I should say, I know him not, I shall be a liar like unto you: but I know him, and keep his saying. **56)** Your father Abraham rejoiced to see my day: and he saw it, and was glad. **57)** Then said the Jews unto him, Thou art not yet fifty years old, and hast thou seen Abraham? **58)** Jesus said unto them, Verily, verily, I say unto you, Before Abraham was, I am.

I pre-date time and lineage. It is up to you to receive, I pre-date even Abraham. This should be an obvious observation.

Genesis 14:

> **18)** And Melchisedec king of Salem brought forth bread and wine: and he was the priest of the most high God. **19)** And he blessed him, and said, Blessed be Abram of the most high God, possessor of heaven and earth: **20)** And blessed be the most high God, which hath delivered thine enemies into thy hand. And he gave him tithes of all.

Aaron's priesthood is the Old Testament. Aaron sinned against Me and made a golden calf. It was then that I made Aaron learn of all My ways. The descendants of Aaron are the Levites. The Levite priesthood and Jesus' teachings are two totally different things, yet from the same source. The Levites did not understand the importance of their task, and they strayed from Me.

Don't follow fools who lean on their own understanding.

They started stealing My portion and not performing tasks according to My Will. Likewise, the false prophets you choose to follow steal from Me. Why build Me a grand building without tending a grand field for Me? I am the High Priest, and no other can stake and take that claim. It is My Spirit that is the true teacher. If a man doesn't come in My name and My Spirit, you are foolish to follow the foolish. A fool is anyone leaning on their own understanding. Would I keep talking about Myself, or would I want to elevate you to being My friend? With this simple fact, it is easy to distinguish My people from the devil's. If you are not loving and in My Spirit, you are not Mine, even though your energy is. You have cut ties from Me and My instructions. Even as I speak to you now, some will still doubt. Some are upset because of their pride, while others are rejoicing in faith. I have given you the keys to understand, if you are being wise or foolish.

Proverbs 9:

> 5) Come, eat of my bread, and drink of the wine which I have mingled. **6)** Forsake the foolish, and live; and go in the way of understanding. 7) He that reproveth a scorner getteth to himself shame: and he that rebuketh a wicked man getteth himself a blot. **8)** Reprove not a scorner, lest he hate thee: rebuke a wise man, and he will love thee. **9)** Give instruction to a wise man, and he will be yet wiser: teach a just man, and he will increase in learning. **10)** The fear of the Lord is the beginning of wisdom: and the knowledge of the holy is understanding. **11)** For by me thy days shall be multiplied, and the years of thy life shall be increased. **12)** If thou be wise, thou shalt be wise for thyself: but if thou scornest, thou alone shalt bear it.

Always choose wisdom and perfection.

Stop being the scorner. You always have a rebuttal for someone who is trying to lead you to Me. You always think someone isn't worthy to deliver My message. Even though you know they are telling the truth. You say, "Yeah, but what about you?" A wise man understands being perfected.

It is not until you want to be perfected that you want Me to return amongst you. It is not until you, who think of yourselves as successful. Understand, there is no success without your fellow man, then will I be able to return.

Love is done in unity, not as an individual. To chase after success without your fellow man is a trick of the devil.

Be successful in My eyes.

You cannot become successful off of your brothers and sisters back and deem yourself as a successful individual. You successfully put yourself above love. Anyone who views themselves above love has ultimately failed. Success is dependent on offering everyone My love. Giving and telling someone something to merely believe in isn't My will. My will is to bless others. My will is to allow everyone to agree in love. It is only when all of you agree in love, can Heaven be manifested on Earth. Man's greed has been the detrimental factor. My children, your ignorance is playing a large part. You are working with and for division. The very thing I am trying to tear down. You so blindly trust man, even though I have told you not to.

Never allow money to corrupt you.

Money has corrupted you and made you follow after mammon. The very thing you chase is the very thing that enslaves you. To pursue another's money is ignorant. To pursue My resources is wise. All the tithes and offerings collected in My name, throughout the world in a month cannot enact My will. You are distracted by the entertainment man's system has offered you. You have allowed them to establish ultimate power. Once you gave power over to money, you took power away from Me. Stop robbing Me of My power! You are trying to fight against odds stacked too high against you. Perform the act of love and build up My kingdom. It is the cornerstone the other builders rejected. It is easy to understand. All these things will be added, when you relate it to love. Out of love, resources have to flow amongst My Children.

Power belongs to Me and only Me.

All power belongs to Me. I am the only one who can be entrusted, because I am all of you. All of you already know right from wrong. There is nothing needed to be said nor debated, when it comes to the right thing to do.

Those of strong faith understand the need to do things the correct way the first time.

"Power to the people" only works if My people have My Spirit. Without My Spirit, My people perish because of a lack of understanding. You are still the head and not the tail. You are still the lender and not the borrower. You must repent and operate as I have instructed you. You will be the leader of yourself, when you start the process of leading yourself. You will be the lender, once you have access to resources. Allow time to build onto My foundation. To build on My foundation, you must first establish a foundation yourself.

Charity releases me!

The foundation must be love and charity. Anything short of that will fail. The foundation must be the countless, otherwise it will fail. The acceptance and the ability to live in harmony with one another lies in admitting, you must have My Spirit. You must admit, you have to be in tune and obedient to My Spirit, as well. Anyone who has become in tune with Me, knows sharing information is a given. You have the technology, the inventions, the machines, the manpower and the willpower.

You must now focus on honoring your true Mother and Father, the ground you walk on and My Energy you possess. Remember, I am, and forever will be, your Spiritual Father. I am the true giver and taker of life. I am the Creator. Release Me once again and your days on Earth will be long. It is only your doubts and fears that separate Us. Trust Me and love one another as I have loved you! Your love is now unlimited and love unlimited makes it unconditional! Your task and goal is to make the world mine once again. Unite and allow My love for you all to reign supreme.

Love, because I have first loved you.

I love you! Now go and love others. The silent whisper that is constantly nudging you in the right direction is Me. It is up to you to accept and acknowledge; I have always been with you. I reign over the just and the unjust alike. Realize, you are My Child. I am there, even when you are first debating going against Me. Never feel cut off from Me. That is the devil playing with your mind. Anytime you feel disconnected from Me, keep your eye on the prize. You must tune in, listen, and obey Me. Follow My commandment to love.

Allow My love for you, and your love for Me, which is invisible, to become visible by loving everyone. I perform the act of love towards you constantly. None of you are worthy of My love. Therefore, none of you are worthy of life itself. You can see the source of your light is and forever will be, Me. My Son, and Savior to all, commanded you to love as He loved. Love because your brothers and sisters are suffering around the world like you. Love is the only thing that can save you all. Trust in it, and never give up hope. Welcome to the fight! Let your light shine! Love without limit! Love unconditionally! Love as I love you! Remember, the ability to say, "I chose love," is better than proclaiming to others to choose love.

The only way for the world to not see Me in it is when you have allowed your lampshade to block My light. You are My vessel. You must put Me on display. Let your love be unconditional and unlimited. Overcome evil with good. Let the world see how mighty My Kingdom and children are. Perform My will. Stand and united in the Holy Spirit. Allow My Spirit to have the fullness of its intended Body. Hold on to faith and understanding. Performing the act of charity is wearing the white robe. To love Me, you must love one another unconditionally and unlimited. You cannot Love Me in the purest form and hate anyone. Purify yourself.

LOVE!!!

Acknowledgements

A special thanks to all of those who have assisted me along the way. Every act of love is always remembered. Thanks, Mary, for everything. Thanks to my parents for raising me to be a free thinker but anchored in the LORD. Thanks to everyone who has put up with me telling them bits and pieces of this story/message to them along my journey. An even greater level of ultimate thanks and gratefulness to Our Father, for guiding and steering me along the way.

About the Author

Although this is Ryan Cann's first book, he doesn't ever intend to write book number two. Throughout this seven-year journey, Ryan takes the time to pour out all of the knowledge, understanding and wisdom God gave him, and gives it to us in a very different but simple and refreshing manner. He explains the Bible in a very understandable and relatable way to the reader. Ryan's message is not from any school or university, neither can it be. It is a lesson in and from the Holy Spirit. Ryan is looking to connect with fellow brothers and sisters in Christ, in order to show the world what our Father's love can do. If you would like to help, join or assist in creating Our Father's Kingdom. You can join me at www.FathersWay143.com. I look forward to working with you all. Much love!!!

@fathersway143 on Instagram Facebook and Twitter

Made in the USA
Monee, IL
08 July 2026